Conscience and Coercion

Ahmadi Muslims and
Orthodoxy in Pakistan

Essay Series 9

Antonio R. Gualtieri

Conscience and Coercion

Ahmadi Muslims and Orthodoxy in Pakistan

Guernica

Montreal, 1989

Antonio D'Alfonso
Guernica Editions Inc.
P.O. Box 633, Station N.D.G.
Montreal (Quebec), Canada H4A 3R1

Legal Deposit — Fourth Quarter
Bibliothèque nationale du Québec and National Library of Canada.

Canadian Cataloguing in Publication Data

Gualtieri, Antonio R., 1931 —
Conscience and coercion : Ahmadi Muslims
and orthodoxy in Pakistan

Included bibliographical references.

(Essay series ; 9)
ISBN 0-920717-41-1

1. Ahmadiyya members — Pakistan. 2. Ahmadiyya — Pakistan.
3. Pakistan — Politics and government. 4. Persecution — Pakistan.

I. Title. II. Series : Essay series (Montréal, Quebec) ; 9.
BP195.A5.G82 1989   297'.86095491   C89-090352-2

Contents

Acknowledgements

I express my gratitude to the many courageous and articulate Ahmadis without whose testimony there would be no book; to Hazrat Mirza Tahir Ahmad, Khalifatul Masih IV who graciously responded to my questions during two long interviews in London and several more in Toronto; to Rahmat Chawdhry who guided me around Pakistan; to Naseem Mahdi, head missionary in Canada who encouraged me to complete my study; to the Canadian Broad Broadcasting Corporation for permission to use an interview from the *Open House* program; to my wife, Peggy, for her uncanny ability to spot my infelicities of language and lapses in logic; to Marilyn Boreham and Lois Lewycky for their skill in typing the numerous drafts required; and to Antonio D'Alfonso of Guernica Editions for expediting the production of this book.

To Peggy and our four,
Julia, Joanna, Mark, Sarah.

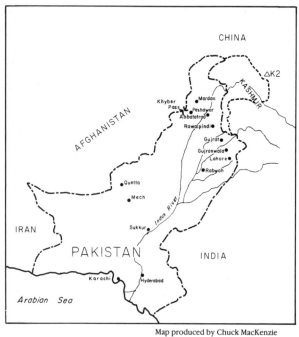

Map produced by Chuck MacKenzie

Ordinance No. XX of 1984

The Gazette of Pakistan.
Islamabad, Thursday, 26 April 1984.

No. F. 17 (1) 84-Pub. The following Ordinance made by the President is hereby published for general information:

An Ordinance
to amend the law to prohibit the Quadiani group, Lahori group and Ahmadis from indulging in anti-Islamic activities

WHEREAS it is expedient to amend the law to prohibit the Quadiani group, Lahori group and Ahmadis from indulging in anti-Islamic activities:

AND WHEREAS the President is satisfied that circumstances exist which render it necessary to take immediate action:

NOW, THEREFORE, in pursuance of the Proclamation of the fifth day of July, 1977, and in exercise of all powers enabling him in that behalf, the President is pleased to make and promulgate the following Ordinance:

PART I.
PRELIMINARY

1. Short title and commencement.

(1) This Ordinance may be called the Anti-Islamic Activities of the Quadiani Group, Lahori Group and Ahmadis (Prohibition and Punishment) Ordinance, 1984.

(2) It shall come into force at once.

2. Ordinance to override orders or decisions of courts.

The provisions of this Ordinance shall have effect notwithstanding any order or decision of any court.

PART II.
AMENDMENT OF THE PAKISTAN PENAL CODE
(Act XLV of 1860)

3. Addition of new sections 298B and 298C, Act XLV of 1860.

In the Pakistan Penal Code (Act XLV of 1860), in Chapter XV, after section 298A, the following new sections shall be added, namely:

"298B. Misuse of epithets, descriptions and titles, etc., reserved for certain holy personages or places.

(1) Any person of the Quadiani group or the Lahori group (who call themselves 'Ahmadis' or by any other name) who by words, either spoken or written, or by visible representation,

(a) refers to, or addresses, any person, other than a Caliph or companion of the Holy Prophet Muhammad (peace be upon him), as *'Ameer-ul-Mumineen,'* *'Khalifa-tul-Mumineen,'* *'Khalifa-tul-Muslimeen,'* *' Sahaabi '* or *'Razi Allah Anho;'*

(b) refers to, or addresses, any person, other than a wife of the Holy Prophet Muhammad (peace be upon him), as *'Ummul-Mumineen'*;

(c) refers to, or addresses, any person, other than a member of the family (*Ahle-bait*) of the Holy Prophet Muhammad (peace be upon him), as *Ahle-bait*; or

(d) refers to, or names, or calls, his place of worship as 'Masjid;'

shall be punished with imprisonment of either description for a term which may extend to three years, and shall also be liable to fine.

(2) Any person of the Quadiani group or Lahori group (who call themselves 'Ahmadis' or by any other name) who by words, either spoken or written, or by visible representation, refers to the mode or form of call to prayers followed by his faith as *'Azan,'* or recites *Azan* as used by the Muslims, shall be punished with imprisonment of either description for a term which may extend to three years, and shall also be liable to fine.

298C. Person of Quadiani group, etc., calling himself a Muslim or preaching or propagating his faith.

Any person of the Quadiani group or the Lahori group (who call themselves 'Ahmadis' or by any other name) who, directly or indirectly, poses himself as a Muslim, or calls, or refers to, his faith as Islam, or preaches or propagates his faith, or invites others to accept his faith, by words, either spoken or written, or by visible representations, or in any manner whatsoever outrages the religious feelings of Muslims, shall be punished with imprisonment of either description for a term which may extend to three years and shall also be liable to fine.. "

1

Introduction
Context and Premises

In my experience, questions for investigation rarely arise from an ethos of scholarly detachment, but out of a personal context of interests and commitments. Accordingly, I find it useful, as a general rule, to ascertain what bees buzz around inside the bonnet of scholars: Why are certain questions asked? Why is a particular program of research undertaken? This is an especially useful procedure when the subject matter is as contentious as in the present study.

The reader can be spared much of the effort of such hermeneutical interrogation if I attempt to cut immediately to some the underlying motivations.

I first learned of the Ahmadis in a seminar conducted by Wilfred Cantwell Smith on "Iman and Islam" at McGill University during the mid-fifties. As part of our task in uncovering an understanding of Muslim faith and the criteria of membership in the Muslim community, we were required to read the then recently published Munir report on disturbances in the Punjab during 1953 in which Ahmadis were the victims of brutal mob violence inspired by conservative *maulvis* or *mullahs* (religious teachers, Muslim clerics). Many of these orthodox religious leaders were aligned with the Ahrar and Jama'at-i-Islami: The Islamic society; a conservative socio-religious movement founded by Maulana Mawdudi in 1941 aiming toward a society governed by Islamic law, and vehemently opposed to the Ahmadis. It was in Justice Munir's catalogue of harassment and atrocity perpetrated against the Ahmadis on the grounds that their belief and practice were unacceptable to Islamic orthodoxy, that I first garnered some sense of this admirable but beleaguered Muslim sect. (I use *sect* in the sociological sense of Ernst Troeltsch and William Mann as a reforming group that rejects accomodation to secular culture and seeks the restoration of the nominally religious community to pure practice and true faith.) However, with the termination of the seminar, my scholarly concern with the Ahmadis also came to an end though, as will become clear, certain orientations, on the study of religion, derived from that seminar have remained.

The next phase in this development did not occur until some twenty years later when, in 1975, I was a member of a small group that trekked up the Baltoro glacier and beyond the base camp of K2 (the world's second highest mountain). The medical doctor of our expedition, Momin Khalifa, is an Ahmadi from Glace Bay, Nova Scotia, and while we slogged together towards K2, he explained the deteriorating plight of the Ahmadis ever since the Constitutional Amendment of 1974 under Zulfiquar Bhutto had legislated the Ahmadis out of their Islamic heritage.

Finally, in November and December of 1987, succumbing to the importunity of Ahmadi friends who pleaded that I undertake an enquiry into the exacerbated persecution going on under the Zia regime, I travelled to Pakistan with Rahmat Chawdhry, a Canadian Ahmadi of Pakistani origin, who assumed the responsibility for shepherding me around Pakaistan. We visited Ahmadi *Jama'ats* (local associations or, as they are sometimes unhappily termed, *chapters*) in the provinces of Punjab, Northwest Frontier, Baluchistan, and Sind.

My observation of the maltreatment of Ahmadis at the hands of mullah-inspired mobs in collusion with government officials, for no other reason than professing and practicing their personal faith as Muslims, was worse than I had imagined. This generated a desire to contribute to the alleviation of that community's plight. Surely, I reflected, if the gaze of the international community were to be directed on to this unjust and cruel state of affairs there would emerge sufficient pressure to reverse the Pakistan government's official policy. What the regime would not do out of moral conviction, it might feel obliged to do out of public humiliation. I am distressed at the delay in the publication of this little testimony, a delay caused, in part, by my difficulty in ascertaining my intended audience. The result is this compromise volume that I am now anxious, in spite of all its shortcomings, to send forth in the hope that its dissemination may go some small way in ameliorating the Ahmadis' lot.

I have not tried to disguise my motive of advocacy behind a screen of scholarly detachment. It is not advocacy of Ahmadyyat, for I am not a member of that community nor do I, because of my own life premises, visualize myself ever becoming one. Rather, it is a plea for elementary human fairness and freedom that would allow the Ahmadis to worship without restraint, to preach and teach without violent disruption, and raise their children without anxiety and peril.

Much of the narrative that follows draws on my diary notes made during my visits in Pakistan. My perceptions are not, however, random but structured by a specific theoretical framework. The Ahmadi experience was viewed as an instance of a general religious phenomenon, namely, that of (1) communal self-definition and (2) external marginalization. This conceptual framework is related to important insights garnered from Wilfred Cantwell Smith. The first is that, regardless of what normative judgement one might personally make about the religious traditions and faith of others, they ought, as a minimal condition of scholarship, to be able to recognize themselves in one's characterizations of them. The second is that the names of religions have historically been given by outsiders, usually as derogatory designations. These orienting perspectives provided much of the background against which my research into the Ahmadis proceeded. Ahmadi self-understanding is unintelligible apart from their fidelity to the *Qur'an*, *Hadith* (traditions relating the precedents set by the prophet Muhammad) and the prophet Muhammad. Over against this Ahmadi self-defini- tion as irrevocably Muslim, stands the heteronomous definition of the orthodox *ulama*, religious scholars — especially of Islamic law — who declare the Ahmadis to be outside the pale, to be non-Muslims because of their doctrinal apostasy, especially on the question of *Khatm-i- nubuwwat* or Finality of the Prophet.

Wilfred Cantwell Smith had explored some of these theoretical issues in *The Meaning and End of Religion*. (He had also written the article on Ahmadyyat for the new edition of the *Encyclopaedia of Islam* as well as an analysis in *Modern Islam in India* that still remains trenchant even after the passage of fifty years). As already noted, he observed that the names of religions are usually given by outsiders and such names usually reflect the pejorative judgement that the outsiders pass on the faith community under observation. The usual name the Ahmadis used to identify themselves was *The Ahmadi Movement in Islam*. Now the dominant environing society guided by the orthodox ulama was redefining them; no matter the Ahmadi protestations or practice, they were to be officially declared *not* Muslims. Even the name that Sunni (majority, orthodox) opponents fre- quently apply to the Ahmadis — Qadiani or Mirzai — carries overtones of contempt. Ahmadis could find a place within Islamic societies only if they accepted the orthodox and governmental definition of themselves as a non-Muslim minority. This excommunication culminated — as we shall see at some length — in General Zia- ul-Haq's notorious military ordinances of April 1984 that were incorporated in the Pakistan Penal Code such as those stipulating that Ahmadi use of traditional Muslim practices and professions, such as uttering the *kalimah* (the Muslim profession of faith in the uniqueness and unity of God and the prophethood of Muhammad), or referring to their house of prayer as a *masjid* (mosque) constituted the crime of feigning to be a Muslim and was subject to penalties prescribed by the criminal code. This was an instance of the historical practice of external definition of a religious group — carried through with a vengeance!

A sense of balance constrains me to acknowledge that Sunni Muslims frequently feel the shoe is on the other foot. Some to whom I have spoken both in Pakistan and Canada are quick to point out that the second Ahmadi *Khalifa*, successor to the founder and head of the community, gave instructions that Ahmadis should not pray behind a non-Ahmadi *imam* (prayer leader) and that non-Ahmadis have been declared to be *kafir* (unbelievers). Although the narrowly circumscribed scope of this study is to put on record the present-day perception of Ahmadis of their own religious and political status in Pakistan, the view from the other side needs at least to be recognized.

The accusation of *kufr* (unbelief) against the Ahmadis seems to have originated in the orthodox ulama's denunciation of the founder Mirza Ghulam Ahmad's (1835-1908) claim to be the Promised Messiah, the Mahdi, and, especially, a prophet. Under the Ahrar (an Islamic religiopolitical group, initially opposed to the formation of Pakistan, marked mainly by their intense anti-Ahmadyya orientation) the excommunication of the Ahmadis from the community of Islam continued unrelievedly. Muhammad Iqbal's *Statesman* article "Qadianis and Orthodox Muslims" of 1934, marked his desertion of his Ahmadi origins; here he enunciated the principle that culminated in the 1974 Constitutional Amendment, namely, that the government "declare the Qadianis [Ahmadis] a separate community."

In the Ahmadis' defence, their understanding of *kufr* or unbelief signified not external and eternal rejection by

God but doctrinal deviancy. Bashiruddin Mahmud Ahmad explained the distinction this way:

> According to our definition of *kufr* the denial of a fundamental doctrine of Islam renders a person *kafir*.... We never go about calling a person *kafir*. It is only when we are compelled in answer to the enquiry of a person to say what we think of him that we have to give expression to our belief... (and) we believe that there exists no such community whose every member is foredoomed to everlasting hell.

(Cited in Lavan, p. 178.)

In addition to narrowly doctrinal matters like revelation, prophecy, and messiahship, matters of social philosophy (and sociology) divide the Ahmadis from the Sunni community. Amongst these factors is the understanding of *jihad* (war in the way of God, or holy war). In the context of the nineteenth-century Hindu renaissance of the Brahmo Samaj, but principally the Arya Samaj, and in the face of the British imperial power, coupled to Christian missionary pressure, orthodox Islamic theologians maintained the principle of literal holy warfare. The Ahmadi founder, on the contrary, espoused non-violent jihad, that is, an inward struggle against personal faithlessness and immorality, and an outward struggle against unbelievers by way of testimony and persuasion. This non-violent interpretation of jihad continues to the present day in the recent book *Murder in the Name of Allah* by the Khalifatul Masih IV, Mirza Tahir Ahmad — the Supreme Head of the Ahmadyya Movement in Islam — which is a rebuttal of western orientalist and orthodox Muslim notions that authentic Islam enjoins conversion by the sword and capital punishment for apostates and blasphemers.

Moreover, in the face of the nationalist sentiment beginning to sweep India in the post-1857 Mutiny period, the founder's loyalty to the British authority was perceived by orthodox opponents as betrayal. As an erstwhile Christian theologian, I find myself intrigued by the affinities between Mirza Ghulam Ahmad's political stance and that of the apostle Paul. In the letters to the Romans, Paul exhorts: "Let every person be subject to the governing authorities. For there is no authority except from God, and those that exist have been instituted by God" (13:1). On the surface these appear startling claims on behalf of the pagan Roman state.

The standard interpretation of this Pauline injunction is that so long as the Roman authority fulfiled its divine mandate of maintaining a structure of law and order, it merited the loyalty of Christians. So long as the *Pax Romana* endured allowing the gospel to be freely preached, so long could it claim civil obedience. It was only when the Roman state began to impose absolutist claims upon conscience in the form of emperor worship, that it became the gory whore of Babylon denounced in the Book of Revelation.

A similar political quietism has characterized the Ahmadis from the beginning. In 1898, Ahmad had written:

> My praises of British rule do not proceed from hypocricy [sic.]... but it is my firm belief that the protection, we enjoy nowadays, by the grace of God, is a Divine protection through the agency of the British rule. To my mind, there can be no stronger proof of the peaceful rule of the British Government than this very fact that the holy movement, of which I am the head, has been inaugurated under its auspices.
>
> (*Kashf-ul-Ghita*, p. 8.)

And again:

> I have also taught my followers to observe true loyalty and submission towards their rulers who have protected their life, property and honour.
>
> (*Kashf-ul-Ghita*, p. 6.)

In the context of growing Indian national feeling, and anti-imperialist anger, such political counsel might readily have seemed like collaborationist behaviour, though the heart of the hostility towards the Ahmadis lies, in my judgement, on the deeper level of two competing communities, each claiming to be the normative embodiment of the Qur'anic way of life.

The founder saw his (and, subsequently, the community's) divine vocation as a three pronged affair. First, God encharged him to reform Islam internally, to purge it of foreign accretions, to purify its practice, to revitalize the spirituality and commitment of Muslims. In fact, until Mirza Ghulam Ahmad's claims expanded to the declaration that God had revealed to him that he was the Promised Messiah and Mahdi, he was regarded even by orthodox theologians as a pious and learned reformer (*mujaddid*) sent by God to renew Islam. Second, he was sent to defend Islam against the external attacks of non-Muslims, notably in the missionary programs of the Hindu Arya Samaj and various Christian bodies. This defence of Islam against external critics typically took the form of heavily attended public debates (*mubahala*) in which divine intervention was invoked to signal the loser of the debate — often in the form of calamity visited upon the unrepentant disputant. Third, Mirza Ghulam Ahmad felt himself and the community that had pledged itself to his leadership to be called to a missionary vocation (*tabligh*). Islam, as revivified by the Promised Messiah, was to be propogated throughout the world. The conclusion is likely that the opposition to Ahmadyyat is motivated in some cases by resentment of the relative success of its highly organized international missionary outreach.

One point of doctrinal opposition between the Ahmadis and Sunni or orthodox ulama is their antithetical views about Jesus Christ. In passing, we may observe that this also has created antagonism between Christians and Ahmadis.

In traditional Christian theology, Jesus is crucified, raised from the dead and then, after forty days, ascends bodily into heaven from whence he will come a second time at the end of history to bring God's kingdom to fulfilment. In Orthodox Islam, it only seems to be Jesus (*al Masih*, the Messiah) who dies on the cross; someone else — either a phantasm or a substitute — is crucified in his stead. Jesus himself is supernaturally raised in physical form to heaven. He will return to earth to exercise God's judgement and, after a forty year period, will die a natural death which precedes the general resurrection of the dead. Ahmadi doctrine resembles the Sunni position by also denying the death of Jesus on the cross, though the explanation is different: The crucifixion of Jesus resulted only in his injury not his death, and he was subsequently nursed back to health. The founder's version of events is as follows:

> Christ, by the grace of God and by the effect of his heartfelt and earnest prayers, was rescued from the ignominious death on the cross, and as in this world one has, necessarily, to make use of physical means, he caused an ointment to be prepared which after-wards went by the name of *Ointment of Jesus*. This ointment speedily cured the wounds caused by im-palement. He never died on the cross but fell into a swoon, which lasted for three days, to serve some Divine purpose.
>
> (*Kashf-ul-Gita*, p. 2.)

Unlike orthodox Muslims, however, the Ahmadis claim that Jesus, rather than being transported physically to heaven, migrated eastward on a preaching mission to the lost tribes of Israel and died a natural death in Kashmir at 120 years of age. His tomb, in their understanding, has been identified in present-day Srinigar.

When Mirza Ghulam Ahmad declared himself to be the Promised Messiah, the Son of Mary, he did not mean he was literally Jesus returned to earth from heaven, for Jesus had, in fact, died a natural human death and was entombed in Kashmir. The Promised Messiah was one who bore the qualities of Jesus; he had "the power and spirit" of Jesus.

To this claim that he was the Promised Messiah (in the metaphorical sense explained above) Ghulam Ahmad added that he was the Mahdi, that is, the rightly guided individual sent by God at the end of time to restore the true Islam, and conquer its enemies and, further, that he was the "reflection" of the Prophet Muhammad in that he envinced many of the same spiritual and moral qualities of Muhammad.

Ghulam Ahmad's understanding of his divinely appointed status and mission was that he combined in his own person the roles of Promised Messiah and Mahdi. However, he gave to these eschatological roles a distinctive interpretation; the restoration, vindication, and expansion of Islam was to be accomplished not by armed jihad but by the peaceful means of preaching and persuasion.

One can readily see why the Ahmadi view of Christ would alienate both orthodox Muslims and Christians. Besides seeming presumptuous, Ahmad's claim to be the Promised Messiah contradicted the Sunnis' interpretation of the Qur'an, so that what seemed to be at issue was the very authority of the Word of God. Christians, whose fundamental theological tenet was that the death of Jesus on the cross was the means by which God atoned for sin and reconciled the world to himself, were logically predisposed to repudiate the Ahmadi teaching that Jesus died a natural death in his old age.

Intriguing as is this novel interpretation of the mission and fate of Jesus, and though it may have figured more prominently at one time in the debates between Ahmadyyat and its critics, it appears not to be a major point of division in the present acrimonious opposition to the Ahmadis. This lies, as I attempt to point out below, in the perceived Ahmadi rejection of the finality of prophecy in Muhammad and in social factors to which I have already alluded.

I turn now to deal with some additional issues concerning my approach in this enquiry into the Ahmadis' experience. Perhaps the most important methodological observation that needs to be made concerns the limited scope of this study. The burden of this study is what may be termed perceptual analysis. That is to say, I have been chiefly concerned to find out how this particular religious community, The Ahmadyya Movement in Islam, understands itself; how it views its origins, its mission, its social organization and way of life and, most of all, how it looks upon the travail of harassment and persecution to which it is presently being subjected because of its faith and practice. The reader should keep in mind that the focus of my enquiry is on this subjective response of the Ahmadi community to its experience of marginalization and abuse in the face of their self-understanding as Muslims.

To this end, I travelled to London and Pakistan in November and December of 1987 and spent this period talking to and living with members of the community at the headquarters in London and dispersed throughout Pakistan in local associations. The information and impressions garnered then have been confirmed or corrected by continuing correspondence and contacts with the Ahmadyya movement in Canada, notably at the Canadian Annual Meeting in Toronto and adjacent centres during June 1989. Most useful in this regard were the five conversations my wife and I were privileged to have with the Khalifa, Mirza Tahir Ahmad, during this Canadian tour that served to supplement the information he had conveyed during my visit to the London headquarters.

It is, of course, always possible that my Ahmadi informants have deliberately misled me; however, anyone who knows Ahmadis knows this construction would be so out of character as to strain credulity. Alternatively, I may have been the victim of unwitting ignorance on the part of my informants who innocently presented myths as literal fact. I am counting on academic training and familiarity with the pertinent background to protect me against egregious errors in this regard. Copies of legal briefs for some of the trials are also a safeguard against misrepresentation.

At the very least, I have presented a faithful picture of the present-day experience, outlook and aspirations of an intriguing and dynamic religious community as they perceive these themselves. I am, however, convinced that on the main question of this book — conscience and coercion in religion — they have provided me with a reliable picture of the actual state of affairs of their community and its relation to the dominant, environing society.

There is a certain imprecision in the use in my title of the term *orthodoxy* to designate the opposition to the Ahmadis in Pakistan. This might suggest that I am conceding the argument to the clerical and governmental opponents of the Ahmadis and acknowledging the heretical nature of their movement. The Ahmadis, in fact, regard their movement as a reformation that repristinates the tradition of the Prophet Muhammad and brings about true Islam. They would hardly understand themselves as heterodox in any normative sense. Quite naturally, I prescind from this Islamic theological debate. In using the term *orthodoxy* to characterize the opposition to Ahmadyyat, I am following a sociological usage to indicate the dominant group who has the power to define (and even impose) standards.

Some readers may well wonder why I have retained in my text the names of my informants. I have discovered on past occasions that religious informants rarely want to disguise their identities and that is probably because they understand religion better than most of the anthropologists who subscribe to the dogma of anonymity. If religion deals with what are regarded as matters of absolute reality and worth, and implies unconditional concern and commitment of the devotee — as I believe it does — then one rightly expects to receive information that has the character of a courageous personal testimony. Of all the scores of Ahmadis with whom I spoke, only one requested to be sheltered by anonymity. As one reads my narrative of the perseverance of Ahmadis in the face of all sorts of physical threats and social liabiities, this point will become clear.

In the second place, I consulted the Supreme Head of the Community, Mirza Tahir Ahmad for guidance on this question. In addition to reinforcing the first point about personal witness to one's faith, he added, with the shrewd insight that must now come naturally to a person entrusted with the welfare of a world wide community of ten million, four million of whom are in Pakistan, that the persons who spoke with me would be best protected by being named. This would apply not only to the Ahmadis but also to the few (unnamed) non-Ahmadis who enter significantly into our account whose identity might be reconstructed.

My text was written before General Zia-ul-Haq's death in an aircraft explosion and crash on 17 August 1988. I considered changing some of my tenses to the past, but have decided to let it stand. Nearly all of the narrative part of this study was composed in the field, so to speak, and I preferred to leave my impressions with whatever sharpness they had at the time. The cases of persecution to which I refer in the narrative that follows, by no means exhaust the record. They should be regarded as specimens of a widespread campaign against the Ahmadis. I have added some interpretive material mainly on doctrinal issues.

It is depressing to note that the trials of the Ahmadis under General Zia have not ended with the accession to power of Benazir Bhutto. The process of persecution seems to have a life of its own independent of changes in the political leadership of Pakistan. This is, I suppose, not to be marvelled at inasmuch as the anti-Ahmadi policy is now entrenched in law.

I am, in some ways, unhappy about having written this book. I fear it being misconstrued as an attack on Pakistan which is, on the face of it, absurd since large numbers of Ahmadis, including the Khalifa, are Pakistanis in origin and culture. In my own case, Pakistan has given me one of the great adventures of my life — the Baltoro Glacier trek to K2 — and other, more modest but equally felicitous times, as with my wife and four children we twice drove across Pakistan. We number Canadian Sunni Muslims of Pakistani provenance amongst our precious friends. My account and judgement should be regarded as the exposure of certain misguided or self-serving Islamic scholars and clerics, and an opportunistic government which perseveres in the dreary and dishonest practice, found lamentably in all times and places, of exploiting religious sensibilities for narrow political advantage.

2

Opposition and Legal Sanctions

The government of Pakistan has endorsed a particular definition of Islam to which the Ahmadis do not conform. As a result, they have been declared to be non-Muslim, their own self-definition notwithstanding.

In addition to the universally normative *shahadda* (profession of the oneness of God and the prophethood of Muhammad), the government has decreed a particular interpretation of the finality of prophetic revelation in Muhammad. All Muslims would assent to the status of Muhammad as seal of the prophets and as bringing to humankind the normative and complete disclosure of God's will. The Ahmadis differ in asserting that the prophetic, revelatory process has continued, not to improve upon or abrogate the Qur'an given to Muhammad, but in order to convey an authoritative interpretation of its meaning and contemporary application. Ahmadi texts and all the Ahmadis with whom I have spoken take care to explain that though the Promised Messiah, Hazrat Mirza Ghulam Ahmad (died 1908), is also a prophet, he is subordinate to Muhammad who alone bears God's definitive revelation to the world.

The Ahmadis perception of themselves is that they affirm, on the one hand, the finality of the revelation to Muhammad in the sense that the Qur'an is normative and complete; on the other hand, they affirm the continuity of prophecy in the sense that the Promised Messiah has had revealed to him the correct interpretation of the Qur'an.

The Ahmadis declare that, unlike Muhammad, Ghulam Ahmad is a prophet *without a law* and *without a book*. It should be noted further that revelation of a lesser degree of importance continues in divine disclosure to the Khalifatul Masih — the Khalifa who carries forward the spiritual headship of the community, viewed as divinely renewed Islam, established by the Promised Messiah in 1889.

The dominant Sunni mullahs and the government find this an unacceptable interpretation of finality. Instead of viewing the Ahmadi position as a mistaken view within the people of Islam, it has declared their views so deviant as to render them non-Muslims. Islam has been so defined that the Ahmadi deviation from the official definition of prophetic finality is regarded as sufficient to disqualify them as Muslims.

The matter, however, is far more complex. The characterization within Islamic history of one religious group as bad Muslims or even kafirs (unbelievers, non-Muslim) is not itself remarkable.

Mirza Ghulam Ahmad, himself, in advancing his mission to purify and renew Islam made extensive and astonishing claims for the necessity of accepting his leadership that seemed to entail condemnation of those who did not. The following passages testify to his self-understanding as Promised Messiah and (qualified) Prophet:

> I am a Prophet of God by way of reflection. Every Muslim is bound to obey me in religious matters and is bound to accept me as the Promised Messiah.
>
> (*Tohfatun Nadawah*, p. 4. Cited in
> Muhammad Zafrullah Khan, p. 136.)

> God Almighty has disclosed to me that whoever has been apprised of my advent and does not accept me is not a Muslim and is accountable to God.
>
> (*Tazkirah*, p. 600. Cited in Khan, p. 137.)

26

These must be understood in a two-fold context. The first is of the entirety of his writings. Alongside these exclusivist sayings there are many others that point to a tolerant attitude of live and let live, leaving judgement, if necessary, to God in the Last Days. This generous-hearted attitude is epitomized by the slogan that is widely dispersed in Ahmadi meeting places and offices:

> Love for All
> Hatred for None.

Secondly, Mirza Ghulam Ahmad's censure of those who reject his mission, must be seen in the Islamic milieu of theological disputation where it appears that *fatawa* (juridical pronouncements) of *kufr* (unbelief) and *irtedad* (apostasy) are commonplace amongst Sunni sects. Thus, Deobandis excommunicate Barellavis; *ahl-i-Hadith* anathematize both. Even Maulana Mawdudi, the arch opponent of the Ahmadis, was declared to be a kafir (unbeliever) by the Sunni Deobandi sect.

Why the charges of apostasy and unbelief should have stuck with such peculiar vehemence and tenacity to the Ahmadis — so that they are singled out in the Pakistan Constitution, the Penal Code and passport and identity card applications — is a problem that seems best resolved, not along the lines of theology, but of sociological theories of class and scape-goat, or psychological explanations of *resentiment*.

Mujeeb-ur-Rahman, who has sacrifically defended Ahmadis caught in the trammels of Pakistan's anti-Ahmadi legal system and was enormously helpful in illuminating the legal aspects of the Ahmadis' plight, shared with me a collection of *fatawa* issued by the ulama of one Sunni group against another (which was returned in kind) that indicated that while accusations of unbelief and apostasy are not uncommon, coercive treatment such as that accorded the Ahmadis is unparallelled.

What is unusual about the present status of Ahmadis in Pakistan is that not only are they excoriated as non-Muslims but they are not permitted to practice what they are. It is a necessary part of Ahmadiyya faith that they be strict in the observance of the five daily prayers, that they pray in their sacred buildings whenever possible, that they recite the Kalimah in their prayers, and in their profession of faith. When they do so, however, they are accused of *posing as Muslims* — a crime punishable by up to three years' imprisonment under military Ordinance XX which has now been integrated into the Pakistan Penal Code.

The concept of *posing as a Muslim* presupposes the competency of government functionaries to ascertain inward motives and intentions, for the notion of "posing" implies doing something hypocritically, doing what is not in integrity with one's true identity and values. But this scrutiny of the heart is patently impossible. In effect, the government adopts the view that it is sufficient to be apprised of the Ahmadis' conviction about the continuity of prophecy in their Promised Messiah in order to decree that a person so believing cannot be acting in good faith when they perform Islamic actions such as offering prayers and attending the mosque.

The Ahmadis seem quite resigned that, under the present mentality of Pakistan's maulvis in collusion with the government, they will be characterized as non-Muslims; what they find impossible to tolerate is that they are refused the right *to define themselves* as Muslims and to practice that divinely commanded way of life which is — apart perhaps from the intensity of its devotion — indistinguishable from that of orthodox Muslims. Their self- designation as Muslims and the practice of their faith implicates them in severe social and legal penalties.

In all this discussion about the absolute and unqualified finality of the prophethood of Muhammad, one might well keep in mind Wilfred Cantwell Smith's analysis of precisely what is entailed in affirming the prophethood of Muhammad. To say that Muhammad is the messenger, or apostle, of God is tantamount to affirming that one looks upon the message that Muhammad bears as authoritative for one's life and which one pledges to obey. This interpretation is consistent with the understanding that Islam's stress falls not on assent with the mind to cognitive propositions but on orthopraxy, that is, correct behaviour in conformity with God's revelation. Otherwise, one might well confront the prospect of Muslims engaging in the same metaphysical speculations about the nature of Muhammad's person as was evinced by Christian discussion about the person of Christ at the Councils of Nicaea and Chalcedon.

The assertion that Muhammad is the Prophet of God is not so much a statement about Muhammad's status in isolation from his prophetic function; it is, rather, an assertion of the existential stance of the one who professes Muhammad's prophethood. Such a person is resolved to live his/her life in accordance with the disclosure of God's will that is borne by Muhammad.

The anti-Ahmadi legislation is epitomized by the following notorious Section 298(c) of the Pakistan Penal Code:

> Any person of the Quadiani group or the Lahori group (who call themselves *Ahmadis* or by any other name), who, directly or indirectly, poses himself as a Muslim, or calls, or refers to, his faith as Islam, or preaches or propagates his faith or invites others to accept his faith, by words, either spoken or written, or by visible representations, or in any manner whatsoever outrages the religious feelings of Muslims, shall be punished with imprisonment of either description for a term which may extend to three years and shall also be liable to fine.

It is under the foregoing Section 298(c) that most of the Ahmadis arrested have been charged and imprisoned. On the surface it is so incredibly unreasonable and malevolent that I analysed it at length to see if it could be interpreted in a milder light so as to soften some of its deleterious impact on the Ahmadis (and, implicity, on one's judgement of the present-day Pakistani justice system).

I discovered, subsequently, that Mujeeb-ur-Rahman, one of the principal advocates for the embattled Ahmadis, had in fact submitted an appeal to the High Court at Quetta in which he argued (in far more adequate legal fashion) some of the same points. Though the arguments would not have abrogated this pernicious anti-Ahmadi legislation, they would have served to reduce the number of specific charges under which Ahmadis could be prosecuted.

Late on my last night in Pakistan before an early morning flight for New York I learned that Mujeeb-ur-Rahman's appeal had been denied. Had his hearing before the High Court in Quetta been successful, it might well have been a landmark for the Ahmadis. They would still have been subject to vicious discriminatory legislation, but at least there would have been some specificity to the kind of charge for which they could be tried.

The range of offences under which they could be prosecuted would have been reduced. One of the difficulties with the hearing before the Quetta justice was that he was only a *pro tem* judge still awaiting confirmation. He may have been under pressure both from the mullahs and from the government to arrive at a finding which suited them. There had, in fact, been demonstrations and sloganeering in Quetta organized by the local mullahs which brought the hearings to a standstill one day. Subsequently, the mullahs were allowed into the Court and sat quietly. What interpretation to put on this is uncertain. It might have meant, on the one hand, that the judge seriously intended to arrive at an impartial decision and would brook no outside interference; it may, on the other hand, have meant that the mullahs had been advised that it was unnecessary for them to launch demonstrations inasmuch as the verdict in their favour was a foregone conclusion.

Let us proceed to an analysis of the Pakistan Penal Code clauses that are directed against the Ahmadis.

I. The word *pose* is ambiguous. It may mean:
1. " present as;" 2. " feign," or " impersonate," that is,

to pretend to be that which one is not. The second sense of "pretend" or "impersonate" is by far the more natural.

II. The interpretation of the single word *or* also affects one's understanding of Section 298(c). *Or* may be: 1. stipulative; 2. disjunctive. If the first *or* in Section 298(c) is stipulative, then the sense is: any Ahmadi who poses himself as a Muslim *by calling* his faith Islam.

Combining *I* and *II* we would have: any Ahmadi who feigns or pretends to be a Muslim by calling his faith Islam shall be punished with imprisonment.

This interpretation would have the merit of limiting the range of crimes under which Ahmadis could be charged.

Ahmadis, of course, deny they are feigning an identity by performing x or y Islamic acts. Through those acts they are expressing their essential selfhood. Moreover, in the absence of a confession, feigning or impersonating is nearly impossible to prove. Therefore the charge is, if not nearly illogical, one which could never be proven: short of the confession that, "I was pretending to be a Muslim when I called my faith Islam but, in truth, I am not."

Even if the first *or* is disjunctive and we have two different sorts of offence, the same strictures apply to the phrase, *poses himself as a Muslim* — the charge of hypocrisy or impersonation could never be proved apart from an accused's confession.

Over against this line of reasoning, the government argues that it is in possession of the normative definition of Islam and that the Ahmadis, because of their *de facto* rejection of the "absolute and unqualified" prophethood of Muhammad, have effectively excluded themselves from the *ummah* or community of Islam. The Constitutional Amendment of 1974 defined Ahmadis as non-Muslims and served to inform Ahmadis of their true religious status in the eyes of Pakistan's officialdom. The excommunicatory move was exacerbated by General Zia's military ordinances of April 1984. Thereafter any Ahmadi's insistence on asserting Muslim identity was to be construed as deliberate impersonation or as a willful attempt to outrage the sensibilities of true Muslims — both of which were defined as crimes.

This raises several critical questions.

1. By what authority does the state arrogate to itself the right to define Islam?

2. How does a particular set of ulama legitimate the claim that its interpretation of Islam, proffered in turn to the government, is the only possible interpretation of Islam?

3. Most importantly, how does the state justify the suppression of a group's or an individual's right to self-definition when no overt anti-social act which might be defined as a criminal offence has been committed?

4. The basic problem remains of the proper way of construing *posing*. If the word retains its sense of " feigning," then this implies a subjective act with the intention of misleading.

Two points are pertinent here.

Firstly, on the evidence of Ahmadi self-definition, this is patently incorrect; the presentation of themselves to the world as Muslims is an integral expression of their faith, that is, their most basic perceptions, values, and commitments.

Secondly, there is no way of proving that another's declarations and actions are hypocritical, that they are a pretense designed to mislead.

If *pose* is merely meant " to adopt a posture of " or "to present oneself as" and if, further, the government claims to be in possession of the normative definition of Islam, then the offence is at least intelligible.

I have not ever seen or heard this interpretation of the phrase *pose himself as a Muslim.* Moreover, we would still be left with the questions of the legitimacy of normative religious definitions by the state.

The legislation which prevents interpretation of the Qur'an that is unacceptable to Muslims on pain of criminal penalties, besides violating the canons of presumptively objective historical scholarship in the

West, also flies in the face of the fact that there are numerous translations of the Qur'an presently in use in Pakistan. Which are to be judged acceptable, and to whom, is an open question which is not as vexing as might at first glance appear inasmuch as the legislation is aimed principally, as most of this offensive discriminatory legislation is, at the Ahmadis.

The crucial charge of posing as a Muslim is a curious one indeed. It shifts the focus from external acts upon which restraining laws normally concentrate onto inward motives so that the judicial authority presumes to know whether the same external acts are prompted by genuine Islamic allegiance or by another loyalty which is defined as *posing*. For example, a Sunni Muslim gives the *azan*, the call to prayer, and so does the Ahmadi Muslim. In the first case, the azan is judged to be legally appropriate and socially correct; in the second case, the azan is judged to be inauthentic, condemning the perpetrator to the charge of posing.

The most sinister feature of Section 298(c) is that it amounts to a kind of Orwellian attempt at thought control. Persons are to be charged and tried not on the basis of alleged anti-social acts, offensive even as the definition of these acts might be, such as calling one's place of worship a mosque. Rather, one is to be tried on the basis of one's inner state of mind or intentions, whether one deliberately intends to mislead or deceive other people with respect to his/her identity as a Muslim. Who can ascertain this short of a confession?

For instance, an Ahmadi could say: "I posted the kalimah in my shop, said the azan, and described myself as a Muslim — only pretending to be a Muslim when in fact I was not all along." In the absence of such a confession, there is no way that an external inquiry can ascertain whether a person's criminal intent was to deceive by misrepresenting himself/herself as a Muslim. Prosecuting such a charge is, in effect, to claim that one has access to the minds of others by means of some kind of ideological electronic brain electrodes.

33

The Pakistan government's present attitude toward the Ahmadis surpasses in severity the attitudes of certain Roman authorities towards nascent Christianity. There the problem was, as evidenced by Pliny's letter to Trajan, whether the Christians were to be prosecuted for specific and universal crimes or whether they were to be prosecuted for the crime of bearing the name alone. Is to be a Christian in itself a crime punishable by the judicial and punitive apparatus of the Roman state, or is a Christian to be sought out for prosecution only when engaging in a specific and overt anti-social act?

Trajan's response to Pliny was that unless there was a complaint, Christians were not to be sought out, were not to be prosecuted for the name of Christ alone, but rather were to be charged only with specific crimes. The situation in Pakistan today is that simply to be an Ahmadi is a crime against the state. The government might desist from this interpretation, but that is the end result of the legislation which makes it an offence to pose as a Muslim.

If Ahmadis insist on behaving in a way that is in integrity with their fundamental perceptions, values and commitments (in a word — with their faith), then such persons will be guilty of an offence. If they are prepared to accept a definition of Ahmadi as non-Muslim and if they are prepared to relinquish those practices, such as the call to prayer and the wearing of the *kalimah tayyabah*, or using particular Qur'anic epitaphs on their tomb stones, then they would be immune to prosecution. This amounts, in effect, to enforced apostasy, to the denial of their self-identity, and to the violation of the particular tenets and practices of their religious tradition.

The Ahmadis cannot deny their Muslim identity because they live under God's revelation in the Qur'an which explicitly calls the name of their revealed religion, Islam. To repudiate their self-designation as Muslims is denying, in effect, their loyalty to the divine author of the Qur'an. This they are not prepared to do on pain of suffering and death.

34

3

Harassment and Persecution

We arrived in Lahore from Rabwah at 11:00 a.m. on Monday, 7 December 1987. We were ushered into the splendid receiving rooms of Hamid Khan — nephew and also son-in-law of the internationally reknowned jurist, Zafrullah Khan. The floors and walls were covered with magnificent Persian rugs and the furniture had Moghul style gilt carving. Chinese vases and screens accented various tables about the room. There then ensued a free-ranging conversation for about the next three hours covering mainly political aspects of the Ahmadi government conflict. Amongst the more interesting points that Hamid made were the following.

A persistent question that I had raised is why Zia cultivates the favour of the mullahs by pursuing their anti-Ahmadi policy. On the one hand, we are informed that the mullahs are not a highly respected class amongst the Pakistan populace. The people turn to the mullahs for the performance of the necessary religious rituals, like leadership at the prayers, funerals and marriages. But, they have no high regard for the intellectual level of the mullahs and are disinclined to trust them in any political leadings. The evidence for this is the fact that the mullahs opposed Jinnah and the creation of the state of Pakistan. They then opposed Bhutto and his People's Party in the elections of 1969-1970, and they opposed

Mujeeb-ur-Rahman in East Pakistan. In every case, the people rejected the guidance of the clerics and voted for the leaders in question. This certainly suggests strongly that the populace is not cowed by the mullahs nor inclined to follow their advice.

On the other hand, we see the spectacle of Zia cultivating the mullahs and using the state apparatus to reinforce the anti-Ahmadi policy which has legally defined them out of the Muslim camp.

The depth of Zia's antagonism towards Ahmadis, and his willingness to implicate the machinery of state in extirpating them, is disclosed in his message to the International Khatm-i-Nubuwwat Conference in London on 4 August 1985:

> In the last few years, in particular, the Government of Pakistan has taken several stringent administrativeand legal measures to prevent the [Ahmadis] from masquerading as Muslims, and from practising various [Islamic rites]. We will... persevere in our efforts to ensure that the cancer of [the Ahmadi faith] is exterminated.

(Cited in Parker, p. 27.)

The problem, of course, is that if the mullahs have only a tenuous hold over the practical and political affairs of the people, how could Zia possibly acquire any political benefit from introducing their Islamic policies, notably their anti-Ahmadi stance, into the very framework of the Pakistan Penal Code?

One of the answers lies along psychological lines. Zia is himself the son of a mullah. It is reported by people in his village that he was ashamed of his origins and would not visit his father's home in his uniform, nor would he even generally visit by day, preferring to go at night when he was not detectable. The effect of Zia's policy has been to raise the status of the mullahs. They have become well paid state functionaries. In raising the social status of the mullahs, Zia has in effect retroactively rehabilitated his own social rank.

Another line of argument holds that such power as the mullahs do exercise over the masses comes not from any intrinsic respect in which the mullahs are held but from a sort of excommunicatory power which they hold. It is reported that the mullahs control behaviour by threatening that the people's marriages will be annulled in the eyes of God if they do certain prohibited actions or fail to do recommended ones. It is reported that a common saying — certainly in the days before the mullahs became paid functionaries of the state — is that left-over food should be given to the village dogs and the village mullah. This suggests that there was no admiration for their learning or piety; rather, their power derived from this capacity to declare marriages invalid.

One of the most persuasive reasons adduced for Zia's exploitation of the mullahs is that, by adopting the Islamic policies of a large and vocal group of the society's religious leaders, he is able to project the impression that he rules the country with the support of the religious leaders. In fact, he rules with the power of the army. The introduction of clerical support masks the true source of Zia's power, provides a propaganda device and, for the unwary, a legitimation of his rule by the authority of the society's religion.

An example of the sort of vocational persecution to which Ahmadis are subjected came to light during a lunch at Hamid's home in Lahore. One of the guests was a man probably in his mid-forties who had been the outstanding graduate of his engineering college in Lahore, the all-time high mark earner. He had received six gold medals. Thereupon, he went to Colorado State University in the U. S. A. for his Master's degree and earned a grade point average of 3. 96 out of four. His department in the Ministry that controls irrigation works — a very important feature of agricultural life in the Punjab — was to send one of their staff off to the United States for a Ph. D. Our fellow luncheon guest was incomparably the best suited. His record, which was forwarded to the Ministry, made him a clear shoo-in for the scholarship. However, to the end of the dossier were added the words: "It should be pointed out that the candidate is an Ahmadi."

The Ministry called in the director of the young man's division and asked why this had been appended. Its presence made it impossible for the Ministry to give him the scholarship in spite of his apparently superior credentials. The director was afraid to send the dossier forward without indicating the religious status of the candidate lest he subsequently be reprimanded for not informing the Ministry of this fact. To be an Ahmadi in present-day Pakistan is to be a non-Muslim; what is worse is that they can be branded as non-Muslims counterfeiting as Muslims, which is a crime against the state.

A further instance of the way the promotion process in the civil service, in the military, and in educational institutions is blocked for Ahmadis may be seen in the experience of a senior member of the Ministry of Education, Shaikh Wahab, the amir of the Islamabad jama'at. He was placed on what is called OSD (On Special Duty) status because he was an Ahmadi. He was by testimony a most competent person within the department, but for seven years he was given an office with no work to do because he was not wanted in senior levels of the Education Ministry. A political judgement was made that it would be too troublesome, especially amongst a population which does not, for the most part, endorse the government's antiAhmadi stance to dismiss him outright. The solution was simply to put him into a career limbo on OSD.

It is alleged that Zia's anti-Ahmadi policy displays a crass political expediency and a remarkable lack of integrity. His wife comes from East Africa of Indian provenance and has Ahmadis amongst her relatives. He himself uses Ahmadi doctors, including eye surgeons and heart specialists. When he became ill abroad, he sent word that his Ahmadi surgeon was to be waiting for him in the ambulance at the airport when he arrived. In spite of this personal confidence in the Ahmadis, he continues to oppose and repress them in order to project himself as a champion of Islam so as to legitimate his power.

We turn now to the question of why the mullahs are in such opposition to the Ahmadis. It must be remembered that the conflict goes back to the days of the founder one hundred years ago when there were polemical debates between Hazrat Mirza and orthodox Islamic theologians. The present opposition of the mullahs is motivated not only by those original theological debates about the finality of prophecy and the status of the Messiah but by additional social factors. Various parties comprising mullahs had opposed the creation of the state of Pakistan. This is true of the Ahrar and the Jama'at-i-Islami. Pakistan was created instead under the impetus of Jinnah and the Muslim League. The displaced religious leaders who had opposed Pakistan found themselves in a country without a cause and without power. In this psychological and social vacuum they resurrected the anti-Ahmadi banner in order to give themselves a status within the state they had opposed.

We visited the Ahmadi mosque in Gujranwala and observed the facade of the mosque where the kalimah, the succinct formula containing the Muslim profession of faith in the unity of God and the prophethood of Muhammad, has been erased by police authorities and repainted by the congregation thirty-five times. The last occurrence of this official effacing of the kalimah was in August 1987. The congregation desisted from repainting because there are criminal cases pending against thirty to forty people. Repainting in this context could be construed as contempt of court. The people are being charged under Section 298(c).

The president of the local congregation, or jama'at, reports that a young man, Munir, was tortured by the police. I asked if the cases against the Ahmadis had been launched mainly by way of harassment or whether they were being actively prosecuted. I was informed that the latter is the case. Since 1974, since the constitutional amendment declaring the Ahmadis to be non-Muslim, thirteen Ahmadis have been killed in their homes and shops in Gujranwala. No one has been charged. This

39

hostility, the Ahmadis reiterate, is of an official sort. Their neighbours have traditionally been, and continue to be, friendly. The non-Ahmadi neighbours do not distance themselves from the Ahmadis for fear of guilt by association. The Ahmadis attend the marriage functions of their non-Ahmadi friends. The Ahmadis own a large field, and the local people use this for their marriage functions, erecting the traditional awnings or *shamyanna*.

Two local Ahmadi mosques have been sealed by the police as a precaution, so they argue, lest their Muslim neighbours be outraged. One of these mosques we subsequently visited. The official harassment has not staunched the movement of converts into the Ahmadyya movement. There have been two hundred converts in Gujranwala since 1974. A convert in the Ahmadi context means an adult who has signed an explicit *ba'it* — a pledge or covenant — in which the basic points of Ahmadi doctrine and the authority of the Promised Messiah and his successor caliphs is also affirmed. Previously they had two mosques. Now they have four and another is under construction.

The Ahmadis have decided not to provoke official retaliation by persisting in calling their places of worship mosques, which is of course illegal under the legislation. Instead, they have recourse to such alternatives as: *Bat-ul-hamd* (house of gratitude), *Bat-ul-zikr* (house of worship), *Bat-ul-noor* (house of light), and *Bat-ul-basharat* (house of glad tidings). I observed that the name on the facade of an Ahmadi mosque in Rabwah, *Masjid al Mahdi* had been altered by obliterating *masjid*.

After leaving the officials of the Gujranwala mosque, we proceeded to the outlying district just off the Grand Trunk road to Rawalpindi, and observed and photographed a small mosque sealed with a padlock. This is one of the devices to which the police and judiciary resort in order to harass the Ahmadis. It is worth noting by way of contrast that this mosque is located immediately adjacent to the shrine of a *pir*, an Islamic saint who is

40

regarded as having powers of mediation and granting of boons.

We proceeded to Gujrat where we observed a quite fine Ahmadi mosque being repainted a bright green by an orthodox congregation who had appropriated the mosque for their own use. The background is this. After the promulgation of the military Ordinance XX, five hundred people, recruited not from Gujrat but from outlying villages, attacked the mosque on the 6 May 1984. They were recruited by the mullahs with the promise that they would be paid a day's labour if they would come in and launch the attack upon the infidel Ahmadis. Only eight Ahmadis were on duty at the time since the attack was launched before the *fajr* early morning prayers. After the mosque was occupied by the Sunnis, the Ahmadis turned to the police for the assertion of their rights which were clearly documented in their deeds of ownership. The judicial solution was to seal the mosque for a month, allowing no one to use it. Thereafter, on 6 June 1984, the mosque was handed over not to its lawful Ahmadi owners but to the orthodox Sunni Muslim opponents of the Ahmadis. The Ahmadis have brought suit in an attempt to recover their property but are not hopeful under the present regime.

They now meet in six dispersed locations — homes in which a room is turned over to be used for prayers. Over eighteen persons have been charged in the Gujrat district, mainly on charges of outraging Muslim sensitivities by wearing the kalimah that is the witness statement in which Muslims profess their faith in the unity of God and the prophethood of Muhammad. Here we may note that although the Ahmadis are flexible and acquiescent in submitting to the legal prohibitions on certain Qur'anic phrases on their tombstones or on the designation of their houses of worship as mosques, one point on which they will not budge is on the kalimah. This, they feel, strikes at the heart of their faith. That is why, when the kalimah is effaced on their mosques, they continually repaint it or replace it and persist in wearing

41

kalimah badges or in displaying the kalimah in their shops or homes as a witness to their faith.

To my frequently reiterated question as to whether the Ahmadis are aware of mass popular feeling of hostility against them, the answer from our host in the modest house where we had tea was in the negative. The opposition and persecution is of an official nature coming from the police and judiciary which, in the Ahmadi perspective, have been dragooned into serving the purposes of the orthodox ulama out of political expediency. Our host, for example, lives in an area surrounded by non-Ahmadis but has never experienced any difficulty whatever. As evidence of the official nature of the opposition, he pointed out that the deputy superintendent of police, the number two police officer in the district, led the first prayers when the expropriated mosque reopened.

Six mosques in all have been closed in the Gujrat district, one in Gujrat city itself and five in the outlying parts of the district. In addition, a new hall which the Ahmadis were in the process of constructing, has had its building permit withdrawn. We have a situation similar to that in Islamabad where the Ahmadis are left with a property whose mosque is only half constructed because the civil authorities will not allow completion of the building. Unlike that in Islamabad, the Gujrat site is not at all usable for worship. In spite of these harassments, there have been two hundred and fifty converts in Gujrat since 1984.

To my question about mullah motivations, the interviewees reinforced what I have heard elsewhere. There is an obvious economic advantage for the clerical class maintaining the present state of affairs and resisting the Ahmadis. First of all, there has been the official elevation of their status where they are ranked as Grade eighteen, the value of which was demonstrated by pointing out that even a junior district commissioner is ranked a Grade eighteen. In addition to their state stipends, there are *ad hoc* fees, especially the *nikah*, or wedding fees. Our host at a recent wedding observed the mullah receiving five hundred rupees. In Lahore we were told that a wedding of important persons commands a fee of five thousand rupees. These are significant sums in an economy where the average wage of a labourer is thirty rupees per day.

This visit in Gujrat brought to light another instance of the type of harassment to which this community is subjected. Our host, probably in his early fifties, was transferred, in spite of a student demonstration on his behalf, from his post as vice principal of a local teacher training college to that of head master of a five- or six-room high school in an outlying village. This illustrates the official strategy which is not only to remove Ahmadis from positions of influence in the Pakistan social structure, but also to break the morale of the community by subjecting them to humiliation. An instance of this humiliation was seen in Lahore where a fast-rising civil servant who was soon to be the head of the state-controlled insurance company was removed from his post. When he began to sell insurance as a private individual, he was so successful that he was told he could not continue unless he became the helper of a junior insurance broker. Control is exercised over the teaching profession by maintaining in the Ministry of Education a list of all teachers throughout Pakistan identified as Ahmadis.

On Saturday, 12 December, I had lunch with a couple of officers from the Islamabad jama'at, including the Amir Shaikh Wahab and a civil servant from the Telegraph and Telephone Department of the Ministry of Communication. He presently enjoys a good post and is, for the time being, secure because of his indispensibility to the system. He was, however, threatened some years back when a German newspaper wrote some articles which exposed the plight of the Ahmadis in Pakistan. Because the man in question, Munir Ahmad Furrukh, had been working with a German colleague for two years, it was assumed that Munir was the source of these, in effect, anti-government articles.

43

Munir had had nothing to do with them. He was summarily sent to a remote village where his special skills acquired in training sessions in China and Germany were not used. After two years, he was summoned back to Islamabad by, ironically, the military, and thereafter reabsorbed into the Telegraph and Telephone Department. For the time being, his story has a happy ending although, as with most Ahmadis, he remains vulnerable.

He did point out that, if the present ordinance pertaining to key posts were applied, he would be out of a job immediately. All civil servants from peon (janitor) to secretary (the number one civil service job in a department) are identified as to religion. Since each department or work section has a mullah permanently attached to it, it is a simple matter to find out where in the particular network there are Ahmadis working who should be dismissed or demoted.

The intimidation also exists at very humble levels. Munir's child was kept from a good school for two years because the child was an Ahmadi. Applications even for such harmless institutions as kindergarten require that the religion of the applicant be shown on the form.

Major Malik (retired) reported his experience of denial of promotion in the army because of his Ahmadi faith. He had had an excellent career record, and had been one of an elite group selected for the staff college at Quetta. He was expecting promotion, but was informed by his commanding officer that on the recommendation of the intelligence branch he was to be superseded permanently, plateaued out at his present rank without any chance of advancement ever.

The reasons contained in the intelligence report were disclosed verbally; namely, that he was a fanatical Ahmadi, and that his constant preachments were causing dissatisfaction and dissension among the ranks. He had never preached or proselytized for his faith within the army. Rather than accept this humiliation, he resigned at age thirty-seven and has since become a prosperous businessman, which he attributes to God's kindness as a reward for his fidelity which cost him his army career. In spite of his economic success in Pakistan, he is emigrating to Canada where he has bought a motel in Perth. He will not risk the humiliation and persecution his children are likely to face if they remain in Pakistan.

Mardan is about a two and a half hour drive from Islamabad in the direction of the Khyber Pass. It has been the scene of some of the most violent anti-Ahmadi agitations. We made the trip on Sunday, 13 December. We parked the car on a commercial street several blocks away from the Ahmadi mosque which was the first object of our interest. Because of events that had transpired there, and which were to be narrated to me in detail shortly afterwards, it was deemed advisable to proceed cautiously — though with an air of casualness — to avoid any altercation — especially since a Sunni mullah lived across the street from the Ahmadi mosque. I sauntered down the side street alone, with my camera pre-focussed and with aperture and shutter speed set since I knew I would have to shoot quickly. What I photographed was not a mosque but a demolition site. The mosque had been not so much razed to the ground as subjected to a pounding that left the remnants of its roofless rooms open to the sky and gaping out into the street past shattered walls. The whole of the resultant excavation was filled with garbage. I shot quickly and departed with a specious nonchalance when the mullah appeared through his gate to stare at me.

The story as I got it from Major Muhammad Akbar Khan (retired) and another half dozen members of the Mardan congregation a short while later at lunch on the veranda of the Major's comfortable home is as follows:

During Id prayers (on 17 August 1986) the police raided the mosque and carted some one hundred Ahmadis off to jail in trucks. They were all detained until very late at night (except Akbar Khan, the president of the local jama'at and two other persons who were held beyond this) on the pretext that their lives were in danger. During this period, from about 8 a.m. till midnight, the eighty-five year old mosque was thoroughly vandalized — carpets torn up, ceiling fans torn down and windows smashed until it eventually reached the state I described above. According to the Ahmadis, the destruction was executed by thirty-five *goondas* (hoodlums) under the supervision of the police. The police took a complaint from the amir (head) of the local Ahmadi community but no investigation was caried out and no arrests were made even though the identity of many of the *goondas* was known. The Mardan Ahmadis now meet for prayers in their members' homes on rotation.

Akbar Khan, at whose house we met, was an intense man with a personal story of persecution for his faith. He is from Hoti, deriving from an old and noble North West Frontier Province family. Following the destruction of their mosque, Akbar Khan and three others were jailed for twenty-six days on the notorious 298(c) charge of posing as Muslims because they had said their prayers. Additionally, Khan was accused of having given the call to prayer even though the azan is not used during Id.

Following a recent court appearance, he was seized by ruffians while moving from the court house to his car parked outside and badly beaten and bloodied. He was charged with distributing Ahmadi pamphlets (which had been planted in his car) and for brandishing a pistol (though he avers that the pistol never left the dash shelf). He was handcuffed and left standing without being offered a chair, which, in terms of the conventions of Pakistan society, was a deliberate humiliation. Neither traditional social position nor military rank (normally powerful emblems of worth in Pakaistan culture) count for anything in pursuit of the anti-Ahmadi vendetta.

Akbar Khan was jailed for forty days in Peshawar in 'c' class — the lowest, where heroin addicts and smugglers are kept. His bail request was rejected by the lower court and at the session court, but finally granted at the provincial High Court.

He is not alone in Mardan in suffering for professing Ahmadi faith. Ahmadi shops have been looted and burned. Still, the local people prefer to do business with Ahmadis because of their honesty, nothwithstanding the preachments of the mullahs against patronizing Ahmadis. Posters have appeared berating Ahmadyyat and exhorting loyal Sunnis: *Don't buy from or sell to Ahmadis*. For the past year and a half, the owner of an electrical shop has been unable to go to his business because it is located in the bazaar area from which Ahmadis are excluded. His business carried on by deputies is, nevertheless, flourishing by his own admission.

In the face of this victimization, the Ahmadi policy remains — on explicit direction from Khalifatul Masih IV — non-retaliation. This restraint is grounded partly on the predeliction for non-violence growing out of the movement's long-time peaceful interpretation of jihad, and partly on prudential calculations. During 1974, some non-Ahmadi young men had exposed themselves to Ahmadi girls. In protection of the girls' honour, Ahmadi youth had retaliated against the perpetrators of this indecency. The result was the 1974 anti-Ahmadi disturbances that spread throughout Pakistan with such calamitous consequences for Ahmadis. In light of this history, the Khalifa has counselled long-suffering and non-retaliation even in the face of severe provocations.

We left Rawalpindi at 11:00 a. m., 15 December, and driving by the Grand Trunk road to Hassan Abdul, we turned north, arriving at Abbottabad at about 1:15 p.m. We went to the home of Sahibzada Sardar Abdul Rashid who represents a respected family from Topi where he was a land-owning farmer until his lands were expropriated for the construction of the Tarbela dam. Most of this discussion ensued on the lawn chairs in the back yard under a pleasant early winter sun.

The first report concerns an occurrence at Mansehra where the police received a complaint from a shopkeeper, instigated by a local mullah, that the accused in question had gone to the adjacent shop and greeted the owner with the customary Islamic greeting: *"Assalam-o-alaikum"* (Peace be upon you). He was then charged under Section 298(c) for posing as a Muslim, it being held that only Muslims are entitled to give this salutation.

Rashid then recounted his own unhappy experiences with the police. On 16 October 1987, he arrived home to find the police awaiting him outside his door. They said that they had been sent to investigate, whereupon he naturally queried what was to be investigated. He then phoned the police station and spoke to the officer in charge, who replied that he had instructions from the station-house officer to investigate whether or not his son is a Qadiani (another term, usually used derogatorily, for Ahmadi). To this Rashid replied: "It is not secret. All the town knows that we are Ahmadis." The context was this. His son was admitted to the local college and, in the column which asks for religion, had written *Muslim*. He should, under the new law, have written *Ahmadi*. He then returned to his home and asked his father what he should do. It was then pointed out to him that he had probably erred. His father said: "Ask your professor to amend it."

The son asked his professor who told him to forget the matter since it was minor. Later, by whatever means, this information was conveyed to a local mullah who first preached against this un-Islamic presence in the town and then approached the District Commissioner who launched an inquiry through the police force. The son gave an affidavit to the local police declaring that he was a Muslim, whereupon the police officer informed the Assistant Commissioner about this.

The District Commissioner ordered the father to appear before him and immediately challenged him: "Why is it that you are known as a Qadiani and your son declares himself on his application to be a Muslim?"

The father, who gave the impression of being a man of indomitable will who stands on his rights and does not make calculating judgements, retorted: " Whoever informed you that the Qadiani are not Muslims?"

This challenge resulted in a further complaint being launched by the police, this time against the father, charging that he conducted prayers in his home, that he distributed pamphlets, and that he preached Ahmadyya doctrine. The two complaints, the son's and the father's, were then sent to another jurisdiction to be dealt with.

On 28 October, the father was again summoned by the Commissioner who informed him that he was creating a law and order problem for him. In addition, the Assistant Commissioner informed the mullahs that they should go to the Commissioner in Abbottabad and insist that if a case were not registered against this family that they would initiate a demonstration, fire the house of the Ahmadis, and kill him and his son. In the face of this, the Commissioner from Abbottabad informed the police authorities that they had better register a case.

The son was arrested on 3 November, under Section 298(c), the charge being *posing as a Muslim*. He was refused bail at the Lower Court and then also at the intermediate Sessions Court. Finally, the High Court on 18 November granted him bail. He is still awaiting his trial.

Another young man who was sitting in our group related his uncle's experience. He had gone to a shop and uttered the greeting: *"Assalam-o-alaikum."*

Someone then launched a complaint that a non-Muslim was pretending to be one. He was charged. Bail was rejected at the Lower and Sessions Courts, and finally granted at the High Court. He was convicted and sentenced to one year of rigorous imprisonment and a thousand rupees fine. This was appealed and he is out on bail pending his appeal.

Another incident concerned the young man's relative who, during Ramadan, was sitting in the common prayers that entail taking only the minimum food during the night hours and sitting in quietude and prayerful attention upon God. A complaint was launched that he was doing what only Muslims are legitimately allowed to do. This meant that he was posing as a Muslim under

Section 298(c). He was charged. Bail was rejected at the Lower and Middle Courts once again. He was convicted and sentenced to two years of rigorous imprisonment and five hundred rupees fine. An appeal was launched and this person is presently out on bail.

During the disturbances following the National Assembly's 1974 promulgation that the Ahmadis are non-Muslims, the mosque in Abbottabad was burned. Subsequently, the local jama'at said their prayers in Rashid's home for the next eleven years. In 1985 the Assistant Commissioner declared that he had received a complaint that Rashid was holding prayers in his home and thus outraging the Muslims. This is also an offence under Section 298(c).

The father replied that he would desist from prayers in his home if he received the order in writing. The order finally did come from the Assistant Commissioner and, as a result, prayers ceased in his home. Prayers are now held in two other houses in Abbottabad.

In Mansehra, five persons whose names appeared as hosts in a wedding invitation were charged with an offence under Section 298(c) because the words, "In the name of God, most Beneficent, ever Merciful," appeared on the wedding invitation card in standard Muslim form, along with the universal proviso attached to any projected undertaking: *Inshallah* (God willing). The young man in our discussion pointed out a case respecting a student in Mansehra who had filled out a form applying for college entrance, indicating that he was a Muslim. He received forty-two days in jail until he received bail. The young man relating the story reported how the kalimah was chisled out of his house wall in a nearby village. From the Ahmadis' point of view, the Muslim greeting is entirely consistent with their most profound faith. It is ludicrous to suggest that when they are using it, they are posing to be that which they are not. This is the absurd nature of the present legislation in Pakistan.

We left Islamabad on the 1:45 p.m. plane, 18 December, and arrived at Quetta at 3:00. Most of the flight was over bare and parched desert with sharp-edged ridges, scree slopes, and brown and tan hills and gullies. The whole impression was one of unrelieved desert until we got closer to Quetta and could observe here and there small patches of adobe housing. Finally, our vista opened out into the large Quetta plain which was still dry but at least had the relief of some human habitation.

The principal purpose of our trip to Baluchistan was to interview some of the Ahmadi prisoners in the Mach jail. I left Quetta with Ihsan Tahir and Rahmat at 9:00, drove through the barren and arid Quetta plain, and saw the possibilities of green landscape in the residues of grass clumps and orchards which shared the general landscape. The rains had not yet come. We arrived at the Sibi Scouts' outpost about 10:45 where we were ushered in and had a very pleasant and courteous visit with a young officer.

Everything proceeded according to the customary Pakistani protocols of courtesy. The servant immediately produced tea and egg sandwiches, a plate of French fried potatoes, and the customary biscuits. A pleasant conversation ensued. Thereafter, the captain ushered us over to the Mach prison, which is notorious for being a maximum security prison from which escape means only insertion into the cauldron of the surrounding desert of the Bolan Pass. We were taken to the superintendent, another very pleasant person with a gracious demeanour. He again offered tea which we declined having just come from the army officer's refreshments.

We sat there and chatted for awhile. It was clear that I was a foreigner and there is no doubt that there are certain difficulties entailed in ushering unknown foreigners into maximum security prisons. As happens so frequently in Pakistan, a friendly and understanding personality can atone for a large number of official obstacles. While we waited, we heard him review the docket of an Afghan prisoner who had received thirty-two years for exploding terrorist bombs in Peshawar.

The Mach prison houses only the most difficult prisoners, most of them *dacoits* (bandits). As I looked past the entrance way of the superintendent's office, I could see prisoners with leg shackles being herded into the large foyer of the gate. In a short while, four men in white *shalwar kameez* (loose pyjama-type trousers and shirt) and white skull caps were ushered in, all of them wearing the most exhuberant smiles. Their greeting to the four of us was in the customary manner, but infused with transparent warmth of feeling and gratitude for our visit. We shook hands and embraced, the embrace usually taking three positions: left shoulder, right shoulder, and then left shoulder again. After the exchange of greetings we were ushered into a room across the foyer where the lieutenant, sporting a magnificent handle-bar mustache, excused himself and left us in privacy.

The following exchange ensued. First of all, I expressed the opinion that judging from their high morale they hardly seemed to be persons who had been imprisoned for one year for simply wearing a badge on their lapel, thus professing their faith in the oneness of God and the prophethood of Muhammad. They replied that they were there because they had been professing their faith in their trusted God and, as a consequence, nothing that was done to them could seem unbearably harsh. When I asked if other prisoners knew they were Ahmadi, the answer was in the affirmative. The prisoners expressed surprise that the Ahmadis were in jail for wearing symbols of their Islamic profession which, to murderers and armed highway robbers, seemed incomprehensibly designated a crime.

The Ahmadis are admired and respected by other prisoners and are treated fairly and congenially by the guards and superintendent; however, at the present time they are in significant measure segregated from other prisoners. Because they are such obviously innocent and harmless persons, they have been moved from the part of the prison housing guards to a solitary confinement area where the four of them share a single cell, which is only eight by twelve feet, but are allowed certain freedom in carrying on their Ahmadi Islamic practices. They pray at the appointed hours five times a day in their cell. Two of them — including the sixty or sixty-five year old man (he is not quite sure how old he is) — work in a prison carpet factory from 7:30 to 3:30; another works in the hospital, and the fourth person works in the prison office.

I asked if the prison is visited by a kind of chaplain mullah, to which they replied that this was the case. I then went on to ask whether the mullah attempted to agitate the prisoners and the staff against the Ahmadis. They replied that that had not happened much, although it had occurred in Quetta where the mullah had even come into the prison distributing anti-Ahmadi pamphlets. The officials in Quetta, sensing that there might possibly be difficulties if not from the prison inmates against the Ahmadis then from the local mullahs, decided to move the prisoners some forty miles away to this maximum security prison at Mach.

On the surface it appears that the Ahmadi prisoners, though separated from their families, have otherwise been allowed decent treatment at the hands of the prison superintendent. It is reported to me that prison food is barely tolerable, but prisoners who can afford it have food brought to them by their families. The Ahmadi community in Quetta supplies their imprisoned members with food from which the prisoners make their evening meal, preparing it over a kerosene burner in their prison cell. I think they interpret their imprisonment and the entailed sufferings as a kind of martyrdom on behalf of God. Although I have not encountered the concept of martyrdom as one that immediately springs to the minds of Ahmadis in explaining their plight (perhaps in apprehension of being associated with the Shi'ite ideas of martyrdom), they did agree that this was a way of explaining their suffering. It is something that they willingly accept, even gratefully accept, because it springs from their fidelity to God. It is a way of showing their love and service to God.

An occasion on which I received an explicit theological interpretation of suffering as not only a

53

martyr's witness but also as a vocation for the sake of others was at the Rabwah headquarters. Mahmud A. Nasir, the principal of the Missionary Training College, in explaining this redemptive interpretation of suffering, quoted these verses of the Qur'an to me:

> You are killing yourself as if being slaughtered with a dull sword because of your sympathy for the people. Happily thou wilt grieve thyself to death because they believe not.
>
> *(Surah al-Shuara*, verses 3 and 4.)

This idea of suffering as a consequence of doing God's work and bearing witness to his revealed truth rather than as a sign of divine displeasure, was also expressed in a parable recounted by Hameed Nasrullah Khan, amir of the Lahore Jama'at. The third Khalifa had likened the world to a wheel that is being driven by violence and which is given another spin by everyone and every nation. God saw that what was needed was a hand to reach out and stop this process and to that end he appointed the Ahmadi community to be such a restraining hand on this cycle of violence.

One of the young prisoners said that he will take up the wearing of the kalimah again upon his release because this is the expression of his faith of which he will not be deprived by anyone. I snapped three photographs of the prisoners hurriedly, although I am quite confident that the lieutenant whose office we were using was aware of this and simply chose to close an eye to it. If this is true, it further evinces the high respect for the Ahmadis amongst the general population.

We took our leave after about half an hour when there were again warm and affectionate farewell words and the customary embracing. They told me that they were grateful for the visit. The single dominant impression was that of the prisoners' good cheer, which seems to be clearly undergirded by their confidence in God and His blessings on those who are faithful.

In response to the earlier question of whether they had been victims of brutality, they replied in the negative, except they said that there had been threats of flogging in Quetta until this was obviated by moving them to Mach. Three of them had received three blows each, but they tended to dismiss these as not contradicting their judgement that they had received decent treatment.

One of the local Ahmadi lawyers who met us upon arrival at the Quetta airport was Ihsan Ul-Haq Khan. He has defended some of the local Ahmadis tried under Section 298(c). He gave me some details of the case which Mujeeb-ur-Rahman from Rawalpindi argued before the Shari'ah Court on whether Section 298(c) is Islamic. The Shari'ah Court Justice conceded four points: 1) the Ahmadis can in fact assert the unity of God; 2) the prophethood of Muhammad; 3) the revelation of God in the Qur'an; and 4) they can act upon that revelation.

This seemed to be a generous concession which would have legitimated Ahmadyyat as an Islamic movement, except that the Shari'ah Court justice then went on to say that these things are done only from the lips and not from the heart; in other words, that the Ahmadis in making these professions are in fact posing as Muslims. This, of course, gets us back to the recurring problem: how does one prove hypocrisy? How can one move from alleged anti-social acts to the interior life of intentions and motives?

The Court argued further that only the Ahmadis wear the kalimah badge. The counter argument was: if it is true that only Ahmadis wear the kalimah, they cannot be posing as Muslims and, by so doing, pretend to be that which they are not.

The Ahmadi mosque in Quetta is sealed and guarded by police. Formerly there was one on the roof as well as one at the gate. I noted only the one at the gate when I visited the sealed building. The congregation now meets in scattered homes, except for the Friday prayers and Id prayers when they meet at the large garden of a private home belonging to Malik. Just two days earlier, Khalid Malik received a notice that the conversion of his house into a place of worship contradicted the terms of the lease of his property in the Cantonment.

I read the draft which is to go to the Cantonment officials, strongly denying that there is any intention of converting the house into a place of worship. Nevertheless, the congregation was reluctant to see Khalid Malik lose his very large and very expensive property (bequeathed to him by his father) through a subterfuge engineered by those who might use the anti-Ahmadi legislation as a means to profit privately. Consequently, the jama'at has desisted from further prayers there. The Ahmadis did ask for the use of a park which is a customary practice, particularly for the large Id prayers, but this was denied on the grounds that nothing was available.

The circumstances of the sealing of the mosque are as follows. According to the police report, on 5 May 1986, just as the prayers were finishing, a large mob of about seven hundred people arrived to — using the words commonly employed here — brick-bat the building and the congregation. They attacked with stones and staves and some were alleged to even be armed with Kalashnikov rifles which are in plentiful supply because of the proximity of the Afghan border, though no shots were fired. The Deputy Commissioner alleged that he apprehended a grave riot— although he waited an hour to do so — and then moved to arrest some forty-five of the Ahmadis instead of the assailants. They were taken to jail where they remained for four days. The Deputy Commissioner required the Ahmadis to vacate their mosque on the grounds that he foresaw public disorder if the Ahmadis continued to meet in their mosque. He had it padlocked and the police are presently guarding it.

I inquired after the composition of the crowd because it would be useful to know whether the membership represented local people who were neighbours of the Ahmadis or whether they were outsiders. As has been testified to be the case on other similar occasions, the crowd was made up of members of anti-Ahmadi movements like the Association for the Protection of the Finality of Prophethood and also from the student wing of the Jama'at-i-Islami, plus some recruits from the Afghan refugee camps who depend for the dispersal of aid monies that have flowed into Pakistan on the Jama'at-i-Islami who have been entrusted with this job, at least in certain areas. During the attack on the mosque, injuries were inflicted upon some of the Ahmadis. The mosque itself sustained damage and is now, in any case, removed from them.

Ihsan's home is one of the homes to which the Ahmadis have moved to conduct their prayers. I have been present on two occasions as the people gathered for prayer and noted that there were a large number, perhaps some seventy-five, for evening prayers — more on the Friday noon prayers. Ihsan has dedicated one large room of his house, which is attached to his study, for the community's use as a prayer room. Across the lane there is another large room and courtyard belonging to his brother where the people meet for prayers. I noted that, unlike the type of persons with whom I have generally been engaged in conversation, the congregation seemed composed of a majority of people belonging to the middle, lower, and working classes. This qualifies the judgement that I have sometimes been tempted to make that the Ahmadis are composed largely of elite, highly educated and sometimes privileged upper and upper middle classes.

At his trial, Ihsan's uncle, the old man whom we visited at Mach prison this morning, said to the Justice: "May God bless you."

He repeated the kalimah to which the justice, in a fit of temper, yelled out: "Another six months."

To this the old man replied: "Thank you."

The latter, however, was not considered to be a legal sentence but an expression of indignation on the part of the justice. The four, including the uncle, who had been sentenced for wearing the kalimah on their clothes, were sentenced for a year and their appeal was rejected. As they moved in handcuffs to their vehicles, they loudly repeated the witness statement of faith: "There is no God but God and Muhammad is His Messenger."

Another old man of about eighty-five, Chaudrhy Muhammad Hyat, was forcibly dragged to the police station by three or four mullahs on the charge that he was wearing the kalimah. This was the first kalimah case to be registered in court and the police were quite stymied. How could they arrest someone for wearing the holy profession of faith of Islam? Nevertheless, the trial proceeded and the defence argued that the kalimah had become like contraband heroin somebody possessed on peril of severe legal penalties. The old man was convicted and sentenced till the rising of the Court because of his age and fined three thousand rupees, which is a substantial fine in Pakistan. A default in payment of the fine would result in a rigorous imprisonment of six months, involving labour and coarse prison clothing and food. The fine was paid.

Evidence of the high regard in which the Ahmadis are generally held can be seen in the fact that Ihsan is one of four elected members of the Bar Council, which is the governing body that handles the disciplinary problems of the lawyers. Khalid Malik, whose large house and garden was a site of prayers until the executive officer issued an order that he desist from the conversion of his home to a mosque, is the president of the Bar Association which is the social organization of the lawyers. Moreover, people had come to express, often regrettably in private, their dismay over the enforcement of the anti-Ahmadi legislation.

One friend of Ihsan's, who belongs to the Jama'at-i-Islami, came to him after parking his car some distance away from his house and confessed that he was ashamed that he had to come as a thief in the night because he had not the moral courage to express his view publicly. While the kalimah prisoners were in jail, they were visited by people (not Ahmadis) who came to express their sympathy. Ihsan, ironically, was hired by one fundamentalist group to defend it against a murder charge brought by another fundamentalist group because it is known that Ahmadis will pursue their duties diligently and with no possibility of corruption.

An amusing and ironical episode encountered by Ihsan was that in Ramadan he happened to poke his head into a room where those lawyers who do not observe the fast can retire to have tea. One of his colleagues said: "Come and have some tea" — to which another replied with humorous irony: "No, he is a kafir and must be fasting."

This displays the amused contempt in which the anti-Ahmadi legislation, which defines Muslims, is held. Ihsan says: "In fact, we are the fundamentalists, not our opponents, especially those from Jama'at-i-Islami." By this he means that Ahmadis seek to order their lives on the basis of the Qur'an and Hadith. He claims that if their opponents could show them from these authoritative sources where the Ahmadis are wrong, they would accept the changes.

Approximately twenty Ahmadis have been killed since 1984, mostly in Sind province where a particular *pir* or holy man near Sukkur by the name of Bair Sharif has incited his fanatical disciples to kill Ahmadis as an Islamic duty. Some of the mob of approximately five to seven hundred who were involved in the storming of the Quetta mosque were possibly from as far away as seventy miles. Some of them were *talib*, religious students of mullahs, whose schools are operated out of state funds. In addition to the groups mentioned earlier, there were also members of the Jama'at-i-Islami Student Organization.

A discussion took place in which I alluded to three students I met while hiking in the Margalla Hills who claimed to be at the same time members of Jama'at-i-Islami and also enemies of Zia whom they thought was not Jama'at-i-Islami but a Muslim Leaguer in cahoots with the Americans, who employed only official mullahs to do his bidding. This contradition was resolved by lawyer

Malik in his agreeing with my suggestion that the explanation might lie in the theory of repressive tolerance whereby a dictatorial state appears to allow freedom of dissent and open condemnation of the head of state but only in order to confuse people and to create the impression that the society is not, in fact, authoritarian but allows free speech. In this case the apparent dissent serves only to reinforce the tyranny of the state.

We left Quetta at 4:30, 19 December, and touched down in Karachi at 5:40. We cleared our baggage by about 6:15 and were met by an Ahmadi lawyer and retired army major who whisked us to the Ahmadi guest house so that we were ensconced by about 6:45. The amir of the Karachi jama'at had gone to Sanghar that day to argue an Ahmadi case where an old man (as they would think) of about sixty years, Mukhtar Ahmad, was charged under Section 295(c) with insulting the Prophet. He had been reciting in the mosque the Durood-Ibrahim, essentially a blessing on the Prophet that beseeches God to grant to Prophet Muhammad and the community that derives from him the same blessings that God had bestowed on Abraham and his prophetic progeny of Isaac and Ishmael, Jacob and Joseph.

The Durood is a part of every prayer that is said by the Muslims during their daily *salat* (five-times-a-day ritual prayers). The amir pointed out that Moses is mentioned in the Qur'an more frequently than is the Prophet Muhammad. I interjected that this Durood prayer is further evidence of how Islam sets itself solidly in a continuous process of revelation that links the divine disclosure to Muhammad with the preceding revelations, particularly in the Jewish and Christian histories.

The accused was overheard thus praying and a charge was laid by Maulvi Ahmad before the police. Initially the police refused to register the complaint, whereupon the maulvi threatened a hunger strike which caused the police to cave in on the justification that the hunger strike would result in a law and order problem. Bail was rejected at the District and Sessions Courts because the crime was judged so heinous, but it was finally granted at the High Court level. The offence is of such a nature that death could be a penalty. Astonishingly, two Ahmadis who are alleged to have simply heard the Durood prayers were charged under the same statute.

The case had simply concerned the confirmation of bail for the accused and the difficult part of trial on the actual charge still lies ahead. In this connection, it should be noted that a large part of the energies of Ahmadi lawyers goes to defending members of their own community charged under the new Draconian legislation that is a legacy of Zia's military ordinances. The amir had reached the guest house just before us and was in the process of receiving members of the community with their various concerns before he came in and talked to us over a cup of tea for about an hour. He had to hurry off to his own studio where he expected to work until 11:00 or midnight on the preparation of his own cases for court the next day. Barrister Beg, who met us at the airport, had been working on three Ahmadi cases in Karachi that day. As a consequence, their own practices suffer in the sense that they are restricted in the number of clients that they can take. Their difficulties are compounded by the fact, as Mr. Beg said: "The judiciary is intimidated by the mullahs."

It strikes me that, though the mullahs have disclosed themselves to be capable of inciting to outright violence, the real hold that they have over the judiciary is through what John Stuart Mill analysed as social control. This means the justices fear being branded as un-Islamic. Maulvi Ahmad had charged that Mukhtar Ahmad, in reciting the Durood, had done something that only genuine Muslims are entitled to do. Since the Ahmadis are not Muslims, according to the Sunni definition endorsed by the Pakistan constitutional amendment of 1974, he charged that they had insulted the Prophet and outraged the feelings of Muslims. It would take a courageous police officer or magistrate to dismiss these accusations as ridiculous.

The inclusion of the two persons on the grounds that they overheard the Durood prayer and thus defamed the Prophet and offended Muslims shows the depth of the malevolence in the present anti-Ahmadi legislation and its application. The amir had argued to the judge: "If the justice had overheard the prayer, would he also be accused?" The judge smiled. The amir went on to say that God gave us a means of sealing our mouths and closing our eyes but no natural apparatus for closing our ears.

The harrying and humiliation of Ahmadis has continued even to the grave. One District Commissioner ordered the removal of a corpse from a common grave after three days on the grounds that the presence of the Ahmadi corpses offended the Muslims whose next-of-kin were buried nearby. This is not an isolated case.

It strikes me that it is impossible that the generosity of spirit with which the Prophet reached out to his defeated Meccan opponents and to Christians and Jews would not have tolerated the Ahmadis. Perhaps they are in error; perhaps they are misguided in their conviction that the finality of Muhammad's prophethood is compatible with their belief in the prophetic role of the Promised Messiah. Even so they do not merit, even on Islamic terms and perhaps one might say especially on Islamic terms, the persecution which has been meted out to them.

It might even be argued that a moral position on the treatment of Ahmadis is a litmus test for Pakistanis just as the Vietnam War was for Americans, and the Palestinian plight is for Jews. I have only the greatest admiration and respect for those Jews who are prepared to go against the stream of the dominant hardline Zionist position and who point out the incompatibility of the present Israeli repudiation of the national right of self-determination of the Palestinians with their self-understanding as Jews grounded in universal moral law. Similarly, Pakistanis are going to have to confront the challenge of where they stand with respect to the regime's unjust and inhuman legislation concerning Ahmadi rights.

We left for Hyderabad about 8:30 a. m., 20 December, driving by the super highway across an absolutely dreary, arid desert of gravel plain and thorn bush and arrived in Hyderabad about two hours later. We went directly to the home of a retired army major and were joined soon after by the amir of the congregation, Nur Ahmad Talpur.

The amir recounted the events concerning the murder of a prominent eye surgeon, Dr. Aqil Bin Abdul Qadar. He had been murdered about 10:30 in the morning while sitting in his car waiting for the door to his garage to be opened for him. The assailant had thrust a dagger into his neck twice and then fled down a lane adjacent to the house. Dr. Aqil was able to back the car up and drive through the gate of the hospital which was directly across the street. He lost control of the car and was dead from loss of blood by the time he reached the operating theatre.

The street on which the murder occurred, and which I photographed, is a very busy thoroughfare with scores of vendors with push-carts and shops. No witnesses came forward to report on the incident nor were any subpoenaed. Dr. Aqil was survived by his wife, two sons, both eye surgeons, and a daughter who is married to a major stationed in Quetta. The FIR (First Information Report) was lodged with the police by the youngest son since the eldest son was away. It named as suspects Pir Abdul Bair Sharif, who is a leader of the fanatical anti-Ahmadi element, and two maulvis who are disciples of the pir. However, the Ahmadis assert that to the best of their knowledge, no interrogation of the maulvis ever took place. The police told the sons in confidence that they had profound sympathy for the family's loss, but deeply regretted that they could do nothing more. The police were instructed by higher authority to close the book on the case.

Some interesting background to the case was also disclosed. The source of information was the amir to whom these events had been narrated by the eldest son, who had learned them directly from his father. About one month before the murder, Dr. Aqil went to the present amir and said: "You are a Sindi and the pir is a Sindi; you understand him better and represent an old Sindi family. Let us both go to the pir's village where you can explain that the threats of murder that he is uttering are not the way of Sind and that he should desist."

The amir disagreed, saying: "He is a criminal. He is a pir only in name and the approach will do no good."

Unknown to the amir, Dr. Aqil then went to a former student of his whom he had taught at the Liaquat Medical College in Hyderabad for many years. The former student is a disciple of the pir, so Dr. Aqil asked him to secure an interview for him with the pir. The student asked: "Why?"

Dr. Aqil responded: "To request him to desist from preaching the killing of Ahmadis."

The extreme nature of the pir's preaching can be seen in that he had called for the murder of President Zia on the grounds that he is a Qadiani (Ahmadi) to which the President was obliged to respond that he was not a Qadiani. The Ahmadis, however, view this story simply as a device to gain nationwide attention for the anti-Ahmadi campaign. In any case, the student replied that he could not get the interview and then added: "I also think that you should be killed because you are an Ahmadi and a defector from Islam."

Dr. Aqil said: "Take a dagger and kill me on the spot."

The student said: "It is up to us to establish the order of priority."

When the eldest son turned and wanted to add the name of the student to the registered complaint, the D. C. declined and said: "As a friend, let me advise that you must not mention these things."

After four months, the younger son who launched the FIR left the country. He was followed shortly after by the older son and by the mother. They have all found political asylum in Norway.

There was a hue and cry from the Medical Association and from the public. The day after the murder, the shops in the bazaar closed as a means of registering both their sorrow and their anger at Dr. Aqil's murder since he was a highly respected and well loved long-time member of the community. Newspaper editorials decried the murder. Subsequently, the government issued an "advice" — it is no longer called censorship, since the nominal end of martial law — to the newspapers telling them to desist from further references to the murder. The existence of this advice was confidentially leaked from the Ministry of Information to the Ahmadis. The District Commissioner said: "I cannot change government policy. I can only allow you arms to protect yourself. That is all that is in my power."

Much of this information was also secured from Dr. Aqil's brother-in-law, Saad Bin Zarif.

The amir said that the congregation has not been dismayed by these murders. He said: "Persecution is inevitable. If we have to die, we will die. We are not alarmed by these things because we trust God."

This is the Ahmadi response to their persecution. They find that their congregations, rather than declining through intimidation and persecution are, in fact, increasing.

The second set of interviews in Hyderabad concerned the murder of Babu Abdul Ghafar who migrated from Cawnpore in India after partition. He was a former amir of the Ahmadi jama'at and about eighty years of age. He was stabbed to death between 12:30 and 1:00 p.m. while sitting on a stool behind the counter of his photography shop. The street, which I photographed, is a very busy one with numerous shops and pedlars' carts. This was a death similar to that of Dr. Aqil Bin Abdul Qadar, a fact upon which the police remarked. Although he had injuries on his hands which indicated an attempt to stave off the attack, the principal cause of death was stab wounds to the neck.

As in all cases of this sort among the Ahmadis, there appeared to be no police investigation, no interrogation of adjacent shopkeepers and pedlars, though this murder occurred only six months after Dr. Aqil's death. The FIR (police report) was launched by the grandson, and the familiar Pir Bair Sharif was again mentioned in the accusation. There was a new District Commissioner; the former one, who had been sympathetic but impotent at the time of Dr. Aqil's death, having been transferred away.

My chief informant in this case was the son-in-law of Babu Abdul Ghafar. He reported that, although it was commonplace for his father-in-law to receive religious disputants from amongst Jews, Christians and Sunni Muslims in his shop, the family had become alarmed by the visit of two maulvis accompanied by two seminarians, none of whom they had ever before seen. These visits were repeated on an almost daily basis in the week before the killing. He warned his father-in-law that these persons seemed ill-intentioned and that he should be careful. They had given Babu Ghafar an Arabic book which he could not read and which was apparently of no significance when its contents were scrutinized later.

The concerned family also began to come to see him daily, hoping to intercept the visits of the maulvis. By chance, the one day they could not come was the day that he was killed. An Ahmadi who used to visit him with frequency discovered the body and, when trying to phone, noticed the phone out of order. Whether this was part of the plot or not the Ahmadis were not certain; in any case, they rang the police from the adjacent shop.

The police came immediately and then milled around and observed for ten minutes before they decided to move him to the hospital. He had in the meantime bled to death in his shop. The knife was left behind. The family did not see the post-mortem reports and, to the best of their knowledge, were not aware of a police investigation. It seemed to them that the Ahmadis could be hunted down on the street and killed like animals without creating any official concern because of the official government line on the Ahmadis.

The most painful interview took place in Karachi when I interviewed Anwar-ul-Haq, the twenty-two-year-old son of Syed Qamrul Haq who was stabbed to death in Sukkur at the age of fifty-four. The father was a school teacher and enroute from his home to the school at about 8:00 a. m. when he was surprised near the school by four or five men and attacked with daggers and hachets. He received some twenty injuries and died on the spot. Also killed was a young Ahmadi man, Sulman, about twenty-one or twenty-two years of age, who was accompanying the father. The site of the murders was the busiest road of the city. There were inevitably numerous witnesses, but no one was interrogated by the police. The son was informed of the attack and arrived within ten minutes, but found his father already dead on the street. Strangely, the police were at the scene. Their promptness surprised the son who suspected collusion since it had been his experience that police rarely arrived so quickly at the scene of a crime.

Dr. Aqil, the eye surgeon murdered in Hyderabad, was this boy's uncle. The father is survived by his widow, three daughters, and this one son. In the days preceding the murder, there had been preaching in the Sunni mosque on the religious duty of killing Ahmadis. The son felt that it was totally the pir's doing. The police did not attempt to ascertain from bystanders the identity of the assailants, but the son felt that many in Sukkur knew their identity since they were rumoured to be professional murderers hired by the mullahs. He himself did not know their identity. The murder took place on the 11 May 1986. The family has subsequently left Sukkur. They departed the day after the father's murder for Rabwah where the father was buried, and thence immediately to Karachi where they are now in a kind of exile, being cared for by the local Ahmadi community.

I then spoke to a brother of the murdered school teacher. His name is Najmal Haq, and he is a practicing lawyer. The first murder of an Ahmadi in Sukkur had taken place in May 1984. The community made representations to the police about the maulvis' plots to kill Ahmadi office bearers. This went unheeded. On 20 January 1985, Nagmul Haq, who was the amir of the congregation, was enroute from his office to his home about 7:00 p.m. He was aware of two persons walking alongside him who suddenly turned and fired two bullets at him and then attacked him with knives. One bullet creased the side of his skull and one lodged in his abdomen. He received ten stab wounds and his right arm, which he showed me by rolling up his sleeve, is withered and retains only partial movement. It bears deep knife scars and surgical scars. The nerves and tendons were obviously severed in the knife attack.

He took a motor rickshaw to the Sukkur Hospital where he spent three weeks. He then came to Karachi where he was hospitalized for two further weeks while he underwent surgery.

Najmul Haq had been a teacher in Sukkur for a dozen years before studying law and entering that profession. He felt that the populace at large were basically against the maulvis and did not share their fanatic hatred for Ahmadis. Therefore, the maulvis launched a bomb plot whose purpose it was to focus communal hatred on the Ahmadis.

Accordingly a fraudulent, conspiratorial eye-witness stated that on 22 May 1985 at the beginning of Ramadan, seven persons entered the historic Sunni mosque of Manzil Gah and threw two bombs which killed two people and injured eleven others. The specious eye-witnesses proceeded to give the precise identity and order of entry into the mosque of these seven persons. Of the seven Ahmadis mentioned in the putative eye witness report, one was in Karachi at the time and arrived in Sukkur only later in the morning (the event took place just before the morning prayer at 4:30 a. m.). Another was in an adjacent district. The third was in Rabwah. The fourth was in Rohri. One of the Qureshi brothers was at his home some distance from the mosque, while the other was at the power station where he was employed. Nasir Ahmad Qureshi, referred to as a professor, teaches at the Teachers' Training College. Before that, he was a teacher of English in a government college. His brother, Rafi Ahmad Qureshi, is an electrician at the thermo-generating station.

This was during the period of martial law, and the administrator called for an intelligence report whose contents were leaked to some members of the Ahmadi community. The report concluded that the murderers could have been anyone except members of the Ahmadi community since that kind of behaviour was totally out of character with their beliefs and way of life. The Ahmadi political philosophy is typically conservative and quietistic. One of the non-theological factors that generated hostility towards the Ahmadis, even in the lifetime of the founder, was precisely this respect for and submission to the political powers that be. An exception to this general disposition to political quietism appears to be Khalifa Mirza Bashir-ud-Din-Ahmad's involvement in the Kashmir agitation of 1931.

Mirza Ghulam Ahmad's deference to the imperial British authority alienated him from the nascent independence movement. The Ahmadis, in their context, may be doctrinally and socially radical; they have never been political revolutionaries and, from the beginning, have rejected a violent interpretation of jihad or holy warfare.

The local superintendent of police conducted his own investigation, which also raised doubts about the story presented by the presumed eye-witness of events. Another superintendent of police was summoned from an outside district and told, in effect, to write a third report which would implicate the Ahmadis. This report was sent to the martial law authority, which pronounced the death sentence on all seven and a fine of 50,000 rupees each. This military court judgement was then sent for confirmation to President Zia who, in a most bizarre way, confirmed the death sentence on two of the seven, the Qureshi brothers. The brothers ironically, according to the fabricated "eye-witness" account, were not the bomb throwers but were in the rear of the procession of seven who entered the mosque.

Following the bombing episode, there was an agitation in Sukkur, demanding the arrest of all Ahmadis. The police arrested twenty-three Ahmadis, including the young man who had told me of his father's murder, and jailed them for about twenty days. The purpose of the bomb plot was to spread anti-Ahmadi demonstrations throughout the country and bring about a general massacre of Ahmadis. That this did not happen is further evidence of the fundamental regard in which Ahmadis are held by most of the Pakistani populace.

There is another peculiarity to this case. It was, according to the documents, finalized on 22 December 1985. It was announced only in March 1986. The Ahmadi surmise, reinforced by some leaked information, is that the confirmation of death was stalled in the President's office for some time and then was issued in such a way as to make it appear that a decision was made before the end of December 1985, when martial law was still in effect. Had the confirmation appeared after the end of martial law, there might have been questions of its legality. The date of issue was falsified in order to get it in under the martial law period where the decision was incontestable. I went to the prison in Sukkur in an attempt to visit Professor Nasir Qureshi who was under sentence of death, but the superintendent courteously but firmly denied me admission unless I were able to produce authorization from the Governor of Sind.

Although I, as a foreigner, was denied entrance to Central Prison, Prof. Qureshi's six year old son, Rahmat Chawdhry, advocate Haq and the local amir — a fine and handsome young man named Latif — were admitted. They found Nasir Qureshi calm and in excellent spirits. He told them: "I am innocent but if God has willed me to sacrifice my life because I am an Ahmadi and because I recognize the Promised Messiah, then I accept his will. I miss my family and my children [he has five sons and two daughters], but I know that God can be trusted."

Professor Qureshi is deeply respected by the prison staff and by the other prisoners. All seem to know he is in jail on a trumped-up charge. His colleagues from the Teachers College used to visit him at first, but they have ceased out of fear of the local orthodox leaders who have accosted them demanding to know why they show sympathy towards an Ahmadi. When Rahmat asked: "What can I do for you?"— Qureshi replied: "Give my *salaam* (greeting of peace) to Khalifatul Masih and convey my request for his prayers."

Only six or seven Ahmadi families remain in Sukkur, the rest having fled to Hyderabad. Young Ahmadis come from Hyderabad to give them protection day and night because a local maulvi, a desciple of Pir Bair Sharif, has preached for the killing of Ahmadis. It is sad to see how this reign of terror diverts much of Ahmadi energies into bare survival and the fulfillment of security obligations towards other members of the community.

When she took office in December 1988, Prime Minister Benazir Bhutto reprieved the death sentences of all condemned prisoners, including four Ahmadis, but they still remain in custody.

An important visit in Rabwah to the cemetery containing thousands of graves of people who had included the Ahmadyya movement in their wills, provided an illustration of another kind of assault to which the Ahmadis are subjected. The deceased had pledged to leave a tenth of their estates to the movement in addition to having given a tenth of their incomes during their lifetimes. Such people are viewed as having made a special sacrificial commitment, so are entitled to be buried there. Also in this cemetery, in a special walled enclosure to prevent vandalism from mullah-incited orthodox Muslims, were the graves of the Khalifas. The inscriptions on the headstones had been effaced at various points where phrases were used in praise of the Khalifa or the Begum (his wife) which the orthodox judge to be appropriate only to the Prophet Muhammad or the companions of the Prophet.

Examples of the erased inscriptions are as follows:

"Allah be pleased with him" — referring to the Khalifatul Masih II;
"Peace be upon him" — referring to the Promised Messiah;
"Leader of the Faithful" — on the tombstones of the second and third Khalifas.

These religious designations had been effaced with white plaster. This had occurred also to other grave stones on which pious phrases respecting the dead had been used which the mullahs judged to be suitable only in an orthodox religious context. The headstone of Mumin Khalifa's father who is, as well, Rahmat's father-in-law, Khalifa Abdur Rahim, one time Home Secretary in the government of Kashmir, has had certain pious phrases plastered over. The penalty for failing to do so could be imprisonment of up to three years for posing as a Muslim.

(I wrote this last part against the background of the call for the *maghreb* or sunset prayers, which came from a Sunni mosque since the Ahmadis are not permitted to give the call to prayer on peril of being charged with the crime of posing to be Muslims which is also liable to three years' imprisonment.)

4

Organization, Piety and Practice

I spent Sunday morning (6 December 1987) in a tour of the Rabwah headquarters of the Ahmadyya movement under the solicitous guidance of Monsoor Khan, Director of the Department of Foreign Affairs. (This is not a political ministry but the bureau charged with conducting the foreign mission work of the Ahmadis throughout the world.)

We started at 9:00 a. m. and continued until 1:30 p.m., going from site to site, from office to office, from facility to facility in order to get some comprehensive sense of the many-faceted work of the movement. We began at one of the hostels, just one of many, but one that is in full-time use throughout the year and also available to guests twenty-four hours a day. We viewed various rooms which were on the model of our own quarters, perhaps not quite as well appointed. Some of them were equipped with two beds; other family rooms were equipped with five single beds in all. Most had an attached bathroom. Some of the larger hostels that are brought into use during the annual convention when some 250,000 people are present at Rabwah use communal bathing and toilet facilities. Some of the new hostels are built around a courtyard. We viewed one hostel that was exclusively for women guests. If they are in the company of other women, they take their meals in an adjoining dining room, the food being brought over from the central kitchen of this particular guest house facility. If they are travelling alone, they take their food in their rooms.

We visited the kitchen which was remarkably clean (I was about to say by subcontinent standards; perhaps by any standards). We visited the bakery where the bakers, with what appeared to be considerable pride, turned the gas on in one of the ovens to show us the operation of making chapatti. This particular bakery had five ovens, but there were nine bakeries in all dispersed throughout Rabwah so that they could produce food for the quarter of a million guests that are here during the annual meeting. We visited the kitchens where a thirty-four burner stove, really consisting of gas lines laid in the concrete floor and emerging at various openings that accommodated large cauldrons, provided food in three hours for three thousand people. Each large cauldron produced food for two hundred to two hundred and fifty people.

One of the saddest features of Indo-Pakistan (apart, of course, from human misery) is the sight of fine facilities such as British period rest houses, and some modern machines, allowed to fall through neglect and sometimes ignorance of operation into dereliction. The discipline, administrative efficiency, and technical competence of the Ahmadi community is obvious in the high state of cleanliness and repair of their physical facilities.

Generally, the Ahmadis accommodate those who come to the hostel. In these present days when they are under severe pressure from the regime, they exercise a little more caution if they have grounds for doubting the genuineness of a particular visitor. In any case, everyone who comes receives food, this being considered a standard part of Islamic, and certainly Ahmadi, hospitality. In nearly all cases, the people who seek accommodation will find it here for several days if they need it at no cost whatsoever. Some who require bus fare to continue on the next stage of the journey are given it by the financial officers of the movement.

From the guest house we went to the general library which houses books in Urdu and English. When checking the card catalogue to see if any of Wilfred Cantwell Smith's books were there, I noted they had at least three copies of *Modern Islam in India* and two copies of *Islam in Modern History*, plus his Iqbal lecture on "Pakistan as an Islamic State." We toured the various facilities of the library. We observed the process of photocopying old volumes which were brittle with age and in danger of being utterly destroyed, and then encasing the originals in a plastic laminate to hold them together. We noted also their book binding facility. Then we moved to the office of Maulvi Dost Muhammad Shahid who is an historian who has devoted the latter part of his life, since 1953, to creating the definitive history of the Ahmadyya movement. He has already completed seventeen volumes, each about six to seven hundred pages. He has published the history up to 1956 and has compiled the history until 1963. He was an extremely courteous and humble person, and I gather from the respect with which he was treated by our hosts that his contribution to the community's sense of heritage and identity is deeply appreciated.

We made our way to the main mosque which accommodates the large congregations for the Friday prayer, the Masjid-i-Aqsa. There we encountered an instance of the malice to which the Ahmadis have been subjected. They were forbidden, after the infamous Ordinance XX by the military government, to amplify their sermons within the precincts of the mosque during the Friday prayer. Given the enormous size of the mosque, which accommodates many thousands so that the whole Ahmadi community can be assembled for the Friday sermon and prayer, the Ahmadis fell back on a system of relaying the preacher's message by a network of speakers dispersed through the congregation who repeated the sermon sentence by sentence. After the lifting of martial law, which has by no means resulted in the diminution of persecution of the Ahmadis, they did reintroduce the amplification which, with a few fits and starts, has continued to the present time. We then visited the grounds of the annual meeting which has not been held since 1983 because of prohibition by the government. This is an enormous field that stretches out behind the mosque. A new property has been acquired to accommodate the annual meeting *(jalsah)* which, it is presumed, would continue to grow in attendance were it free of restraint from the government. The institution of the annual meeting was inaugurated by the founder himself. The Ahmadis clearly attach a great deal of importance to this vast assembly of all the faithful who can possibly be present.

We next visited the training college for missionaries. We looked into a classroom which had standard college-type furniture, and moved on to the college library which, after quick surveillance, appeared to be highly eclectic ranging from Kipling's *Captains' Courageous* and Hemingway's stories to Elliot's two-volume work on Hinduism and Buddhism, and translations of the Bible. The curriculum consists of Urdu and Arabic language, Qur'an, Hadith, and comparative religions. When I inquired after the nature of the comparative religion curriculum, the principal informed me that they did not rely much on secondary sources, but rather on primary material like the scriptures of the traditions. I later asked a group of foreign students how they studied comparative religions. This group consisted of three or four Ugandans, one Nigerian, one from the Ivory Coast, one American black (Ahmadi by birth) and one Englishman (a white convert). Several other blacks came along subsequently when they saw us clustering. I could not be certain of their origins, most probably West Africa since the Ahmadis exist there in strength. I was told by a Ugandan, who spoke excellent English and seemed to have an outstanding ability to articulate what he was doing, that they studied other religions mainly through the works of the Promised Messiah and the second Khalifa who wrote particularly on Christianity.

Having received the correct orientation on other traditions, they would then look at some of the scriptures of Christianity and Judaism in confirmation and instantiation of the insights and judgements promulgated by the leaders of the Ahmadi community. This style of comparative religion — so different from what is pursued in our Western universities — is explained, as the principal said, by the fact that they know themselves to be in possession of the truth and, therefore, see their primary responsibility as expositing that given truth and relating it to other areas of inquiry.

The Ahmadyya missionary training course at Rabwah is of either three or five years' duration, to which is added in each case an additional year of practical instruction ranging over such subjects as Bookkeeping, Typing and Electrical Maintenance. Students entering with over seventy-five percent in their matriculation would take the five-year course. Those already holding a degree are given varying amounts of credit, depending on their previous area of study. Those with a degree in Arabic Literature, for example, would get a higher advanced standing than someone with a degree in engineering. Two young men, now on permanent staff, come from backgrounds as practicing lawyer and history lecturer.

The criteria for selection are not only academic, but also moral and devotional. Here the college depends upon reports provided by the applicant's home jama'at or congregation. The enrollment this year is eighty-three students out of ninety applicants. Each applicant is interviewed to ascertain that he has a true vocation for the mission field and is not simply acquiescing to paternal desires.

The curriculum covers Urdu language (which is the main medium of instruction), Arabic, Hadith, and Comparative Religion. No attempt is made to target certain religious traditions so that a missionary becomes an expert, for example, in relating the Ahmadi Muslim message to Christians or animists. It is assumed that a missionary ought to be able to deal with the mentality and enquiries of whomsoever he approaches in the geographical area to which he is sent.

Students previously came to Rabwah from various parts of the world, including heavy enrolments from Indonesia and West Africa. Nowadays, the refusal or reluctance of the Pakistan government to grant entrance visas to foreign Ahmadi students has meant the disappearance or reduction of this foreign component. As a result, the movement has opened other training centres abroad, including one in West Africa.

Upon graduation, the students make a life commitment to the mission work of the movement.

During tea on the veranda of the Rabwah Missionary Training College with the principal, I had the opportunity to pose some doctrinal questions about the precise nature of his understanding of the relation of the Qur'anic revelation to preceding revelations. My question specifically was: "Did Muhammad recapitulate in an Arabic form for the Arab peoples and, through them, to the world, the original revelations given to Adam, Moses, David and Jesus, or did Muhammad bring new truth which had not heretofore been disclosed by God to other prophets?"

There is little debate concerning the Muslims' understanding of the relation of the Qur'an to existing revelations or other holy books because these are viewed as distorted residues of the original revelations—distorted by omissions, additions or changes in meaning. With respect to extant revelations, the Qur'anic revelation clearly fulfils them in the sense that it confirms the partial truths they still contain and supplies the truth that they have lost in the course of history.

The crux of my question was the relation of the Qur'an to the *original* disclosures to other prophets. Here the answer also lay along the lines of fulfilment theory. In essentials, the religious message remains the same. God has one religion which He gave to Adam and, subsequently, reiterated to successive prophets through the ages. The Qur'an, however, does not only recapitulate that primordial divine religion; it also fulfils it by giving information from God that was not heretofore disclosed because it was not required. The message in the Qur'an is the message, the college principal stressed, for the present age — this present historical epoch— until the day of judgment. For this period, God reveals things that were not pertinent before, including such things as space travel (which the principal finds in embryonic form in the Qur'an), and present-day discoveries in genetics.

In sum, the Qur'an repeats the original disclosures and, moreover, provides an addendum that was not disclosed to earlier prophets because it was not needed in their times.

Naseem Saifi, Director of Education of the Jammia Ahmadiyya, expressed similar views on the Islamic understanding of revelation. As I interpret his position, the conceptual category that best accommodates the Ahmadi Muslim view of other religions is *fulfilment*. In their origins, all other traditions had a revelation, a book, from God. Through the passage of time, however, the other religious communities have allowed omissions, additions, and distortions to creep in, with the result that their revealed books now contain only partial truth. God in his mercy has sent the Qur'an to the Prophet Muhammad, which contains all the truth that the other historically perverted traditions now contain only in part. The Qur'an confirms and fulfils, or completes, the partial truth of other religious traditions.

Thereafter, we drove by a kind of law court which serves to adjudicate civil conflicts within the Ahmadi community. It is thought both injurious to the sense of community and economically damaging to have Ahmadis take their conflicts to state courts. As far as is possible, parties to conflicts appear before a rotating board of judges who listen to both sides and then adjudicate the matter. The recourse to this style of court is on a purely voluntary basis.

Finally, we visited a new housing project that the Ahmadis are building adjacent to the newly acquired site for their annual meeting. For their centenary project marking the one hundredth anniversary since the founding of the movement in 1889 by Hazrat Mirza Ghulam Ahmad, the Ahmadis are building one hundred houses to be given to poor people. Eighty are two-bedroom construction and twenty are three- bedroom construction. They are solidly built brick structures with foundations going down four or five feet, a thickness of wall of approximately eighteen inches, and waterproofed at three points by bitumen in order to prevent dampness from seeping into the houses. They contain a bathroom, a storeroom, a kitchen, and two or three bedrooms. These houses, as almost all the buildings at Rabwah, are designed by a committee of Ahmadi architects who volunteer their time to the community and to the service of God. There is a nearby artesian well gushing forth very great amounts of fresh water, so it is visualized that this will in due course be a thriving community of poor people drawn — originally at least — from Ahmadi ranks who will be handed over the keys in 1989.

In response to my question of how the community manages to maintain the momentum of its original inspiration, Monsoor Khan replied that this is the role of the Khalifa. The personal dynamic that generated the devotion of the original devotees at the time of the founder, the Promised Messiah, is now continued in the life of the commuity by the Khalifatul Masih who, after his election to the office as Khalifa, or successor, to the Promised Messiah, is understood to possess a special charisma, or grace, that draws him closer to God and the community to God through him. Consequently, the community continues to have a special personal loyalty focused on the figure of the Khalifa that inspires devotion and commitment to ongoing service for God and for the community. This might be exemplified by an event that occurred to Rahmat this afternoon at prayers. Arriving some fifteen minutes before prayers, he was met by two elderly men who asked: "Have you just come from London?"

He replied: "Yes."

They asked: "Did you see Khalifatul Masih?"

Rahmat said that we had had two long sessions with the spiritual leader. They both seemed pleased that they could make contact with someone who had so recently touched the hem of the garment of their beloved leader and, at the same time, were pained that the present discriminatory policies of the regime made it impossible for the Khalifatul Masih to carry on his work in the Rabwah headquarters.

The following episodes are intended to illustrate the mentality of the Ahmadis with whom I have been travelling, explicitly with respect to their confidence in the providential guidance of God in all events, both great and important events relating to the plight of their fidelity under the present regime, and also the homely everyday occurrences of their lives.

Iftikhar related how on one occasion late in the evening his eight-year-old daughter asked if she could invite some school friends in for a party the next day. Her father replied that it was all right but, at the same time, he hesitated in that he found himself with no money whatsoever and would be unable to buy the necessary food to provide the party. As was his custom he prayed: "Dear God, I have been faithful. I love You. I pray to You to do Your will. Help me now. Please God, send me some money so that I can provide this party for my daughter who asks me for very little, but has asked me for this one thing."

It was late at night, getting close to midnight, when there was an insistent knock at the gate by one of the brother's friends and customers. He reported that he was on his way to the airport to his job in Denmark and he wanted three sets of fur cushions which were for sale in the brother's business. Iftikhar was able to secure these and pass them on at six hundred rupees per set. With this money providentially sent, as Iftikhar believes, he was able to purchase the festive foodstuffs that were required for his daughter's party. God had graciously intervened to allow his brother to advance him the necessary money.

Rahmat reports an episode pertaining to his daughter Samina's wedding in Pakistan. Although Ahmadi weddings are very simple relative to other Muslim weddings in that the Ahmadis reject the enormous expenditures that are customarily assumed by the families in providing dowries and enormous feasts for invited guests, they nevertheless follow the Pakistani custom of providing the bride with a part of her inheritance in the form of gold jewellery. Rahmat had purchased what I gathered was a very expensive amount of jewellery which he had consigned to the safety deposit vault at an Islamabad bank. During tea on the afternoon several days before the wedding, he learned from his guests that Id holidays had already started and that everything would be closed up tight for four days, including the day of his daughter's wedding. This meant he was unable to give her the wedding jewellery, which he felt was a devastating failure on his part. He felt that he had failed this daughter, who had never given any trouble, on the occasion of her wedding. He prayed: "Please God, help me to secure this jewellery. Help me get the jewellery out of the bank vault."

He phoned the manager who invited him over to his house and then patiently and kindly explained that there was absolutely nothing that could be done. When the bank vault was closed, that was it for the night.

Rahmat persisted and there unfolded a long and complex story which I cannot relate in detail. It involved the five persons who are required to get into the bank at night plus the consent of the shotgun-wielding guard who is not directly answerable to the bank manager. Since the holidays had started, the five functionaries involved were dispersed. Nevertheless, Rahmat accomplished that which is normally simply impossible, namely, entry into the vault at about two o'clock in the morning. He drove around Islamabad and Rawalpindi locating people in their homes, in a shoe store, and on the verge of departing for their distant villages for the holiday. Finally, in the middle of the night, he got them all assembled at the bank with their respective keys to gain access to his jewellery in the vault. He was thus able to fulfill his paternal duty and present his daughter on her wedding with the customary Pakistani gold jewellery. He reports that to this day the bank manager, when he sees him, scarcely wants to speak to him and says: "Listen, don't ever talk to me about letting you into the bank. I don't know why I did it. I don't even want to discuss it. I want to pretend it never occurred."

I am not able to comment on the intricacies of Pakistani banking procedures, but I can report my informant's understanding of the situation, namely, that the events of that night simply could not, in principle, happen. Why it should have occurred on this occasion Rahmat can explain only in terms of divine grace. God was once again being good to him, showering him with His mercy so that there could be a happy wedding.

Another episode concerns the afternoon when we went shopping for old Afghan and Baluchi tribal jewellery for my wife and daughters in the Rawalpindi market. After much haggling, producing very little discount, we arrived at a price of two thousand six hundred and fifty rupees. I did not have this much money with me, nor did Rahmat. We gave the shopkeeper six hundred rupees, whereupon he gave the jewellery to us with an indication that the rest of the money could be paid to a relative's shop in Islamabad.

This again was an unheard of procedure. Rahmat had proposed having the store's boy come with us in the car back to Islamabad, whereupon he would hand over the balance of the money. The shopkeeper said: "It is not necessary. You have an honest face. You look like you are incapable of telling a lie. I trust that you will deliver the money to my relative in Islamabad this afternoon."

This arrangement certainly was convenient for us; Rahmat remained astonished by this way of acting. His interpretation of the event was that it was one further instance of God's supreme kindness to those who love

Him and seek to follow Him. In his terms, this meant committing their lives to the Ahmadi belief and practice.

The Ahmadis that I have travelled with have a remarkable confidence in the reality and providence of God. They take it for granted that God intervenes, even in their everyday affairs, to bring good issue out of their dilemmas in response to their trust and fidelity in Him.

Iftikhar records another experience of a wedding party. Two elderly aunts had been invited from outside the city. They arrived at the home in a taxi and took all their bundles except one, the most precious, namely, the family jewellery which they had wrapped in cloth and carried with them for safekeeping on their travel from their village. Soon after entering the house, they discovered the absence of this cloth-wrapped bundle and Iftikhar and a cousin went out in their own car and began to drive aimlessly (non-believers might say) to see if they might find the taxi in question. They began this pursuit without any knowledge at all of the number of the taxi or the direction in which it might have headed. By their account, they took eleven different turns, some left, some right, and finally came upon a taxi parked in front of a food stall where the driver had gone for his meal. They approached the taxi to inquire and, looking in on the back seat, espied the cloth bundle. They quickly retrieved it and spoke to the taxi driver who had realized it was there but had not yet taken any initiative to ascertain its contents. When Iftikhar and the cousin approached, he said: "I told those old ladies to take their bundle."

He then related how someone had stopped him for a lift, but he had simply refused the fare, saying he was tired and hungry and he was going to stop for some food. The assumption is that had the fare been picked up, the cloth bundle would have disappeared with the passenger. The retrieval of this lost jewellery under these circumstances strikes Iftikhar and his family as being so incredible that it can be understood only as the guidance of God who intervenes to do good things for His faithful

84

people. One must remark that the degree of synchronicity in the unfolding of this story is so remarkable that it is almost easier to accept the assumption that a divine providence is at work than to ascribe the results to chance.

If one understands the role that jewellery plays in Pakistan culture as moveable assets that can be transported in times of disaster, and as easily transmitted legacies which parents bequeath to children, then one will understand the importance of this episode. The happy results of what would have otherwise been experienced as a calamity, Iftikhar ascribes only to God's guidance, leading and kindness. Those events, which might seem inadvertent to outsiders, were the consequence of the promptings of God. This event is one amongst a large number that the Ahmadis in question can produce as demonstrations in their own lives of the goodness of God, His power, and His mercy.

On the morning that we left Rawalpindi by car for Abbottabad, the customary prayer beseeching God's protection on our journey in fulfillment of His will, and to do His work, was given just before our departure. Iftikhar (who is employed by a small independent bank) then reported that each morning when he sits in his car he thanks God that, whereas before he was searching and searching for Him, now he had found Him. Then he thanks God for his car (new Suzuki mini-van). Also he went on to point out how God is responsible for all the good things that happen to him.

It must be borne in mind that Iftikhar expressed himself in a foreign language, English, which makes it impossible for him to render the nuances he might want. Nevertheless, this is consistent with most of the testimony I heard that looks upon material, this-worldly, blessings as a natural consequence of a Muslim's devotion in the service of God.

A retired Group Captain reported over tea and after lunch in Rawalpindi that "the main difference between us and our competitors is that we believe in a living God.

When we call, He responds; when we demand, He gives." This theme of Ahmadi reliance on a living God was one which I was to hear on a numerous occasions.

This attitude of unquestioning trust in God's guidance and God's reward of the faithful extends from the simple domestic affairs we have narrated to weighty matters of war and politics. General Ali Malik told me of his feelings during the battle at Chowindah that began 8 September 1965 in which his fighting group of one infantry battalion and one armoured regiment intercepted an invading Indian army of four infantry battalions and four armoured regiments. The possibility was strong that were the Indian army to break through, Pakistan would fall. The ensuing battle lasted three days and nights. In explaining the Pakistan victory, General Malik said: "God takes control of minds. God helps his favoured people by putting fear into the minds of the enemy. This was one of those cases. God helped me because I'm an Ahmadi. I was only God's instrument."

The starkness of Ahmadi confidence in God's active guidance is evident in all strata of their membership.

In June of 1974, General Malik received a letter informing him that he would be retired effective September of 1974 even though he still had three years to go until retirement. In the normal course of events he would likely have succeeded to the Chief of Staff. He remains quite certain that he was retired prematurely because he is an Ahmadi.

So often it has seemed to me that the divine response that Ahmadis expect is in material "this worldly" terms. This discernment of a causal connection between faith in God and material prosperity (along the lines of Max Weber's analysis of late Calvinism's conviction that worldly blessings were a sign of God's election) is not, however, the whole of Ahmadian theodicy. The Group Captain in Rawalpindi made it clear that, although these material benefits were also expected and frequently given, the benefit that was never denied was that of inward peace of mind. The question of eschatological benefits in heaven did not receive the amount of stress that I would have expected, although our banker host did compare eschatological awards to fixed accounts where the benefits are enjoyed in the future, in heaven.

As I point out elsewhere, there is another co-existing strand that recognizes that the price of fidelity and obedience to God is often suffering. Given the Ahmadis experience of persecution for their uncompromisable religious stance, this other self-sacrificing, passion motif could hardly be obscured.

The Group Captain, Abdul Shakur Malik, was denied an expected extension of service when he reached retirement age at fifty-one. He had every expectation that he would serve for at least another three years. He was personally and confidentially told that an extension was denied because he is an Ahmadi.

My Canadian travelling companion, Rahmat, after twenty-three years' in the Pakistan military service, had his military career terminated because, as a letter in his file confidentially indicated, he was an Ahmadi whose preaching was disruptive. (He did not preach at all, though his life style — abstention from alcohol in the mess, the foreswearing of womanizing — set him and other Ahmadis apart and often generated resentment.) It must be borne in mind that these men served when alcohol was a part of Pakistan military life. The drying out of military messes began in the late sixties and early seventies.

The dominant image of Islam in the West is one of dogmatic beliefs and inflexible practice, an impression which needs some correction. When I was interviewing three directors of the Ahmadi organizations at their Rabwah headquarters, I was faintly aware of the *maghreb* (sunset) call to prayer but, being deep in discussion, its significance did not register. Only later did it break in upon me that I had kept the three from their prayers. Upon my apology, they explained that no harm had been done because, if an appointed prayer has been missed due to some duty or other inability, they are permitted to join the missed prayer to another later one. In this case, their hospitality to me, a guest, justified their foregoing the *maghreb* prayer; it would later accompany their *isha* (late night prayer).

Only stubborn orthodox mullahs, in the judgement of my Ahmadi informants, would insist on stopping a bus full of passengers fifteen minutes from its destination, at the end of the two hundred mile run from Lahore to Rawalpindi, in order that they might ostentatiously display their piety in public prayer. Genuine Islamic practice, so they argued, would have permitted the mullahs to say their prayers on the bus during travel, or to join them with the subsequent prayer period.

I had a most interesting and informative conversation with the barrister who picked us up at the Karachi airport after our flight from Quetta. When I went into the guest house room to which I had been assigned, I noted that he was actively assisting his own house servant in the clean-up of the toilet in preparation for my occupation of the quarters. I could not help but remark to him how out of character this was in that one does not normally find in the subcontinent professional people involved in the cleaning of toilets. I further remarked that this seemed to be characteristic of Ahmadis in that the faith has produced a kind of social transformation in which the strict hierarchical divisions of status and labour which avail generally throughout Indo-Pakistan society are heavily modified in the direction of an egalitarian brotherhood. As it turned out, the servant who has been with the barrister since he was a young boy of twelve is not an Ahmadi but a Sunni Pathan, but has indicated his desire to become an Ahmadi.

My observation introduced some further comments from the barrister. He pointed out that it is an Ahmadi's part to work with one's hands. In fact, within the last week, he and a number of other Ahmadis whitewashed the mosque with their own hands. In Pakistan society this is quite unusual, in contrast to the Canadian Protestant church context with its tradition of work camps and congregational bees. Yet, even within the Canadian church context, it would be increasingly difficult to conscript the professional classes in the average middle-class congregation for work parties of this sort since the tendency, as I discern it nowadays, is to assign these jobs to professionals.

He further remarked that the servant girl who lives with them is a Christian but is treated as a member of the family. His wife, before going up to their home in the Punjab a few days ago, had gone to the bazaar and bought, for the girl, a new dress, bangles, shoes and tops for the girl, which she wrapped to be given to her on Christmas eve. Though in Pakistan it is unheard of for people to drink from the same glass from which the sweeper drinks, in his household there are no distinctions in dining or use of utensils.

Ahmadis are different people than most of the environing society. That is why they can so frequently recognize one another instinctively in the crowded airports or train stations. He said that Ahmadis, no matter how poor they are, tend to dress differently in the sense that their clothes and their persons are clean even if the garments are the simple ones of poor folk. The educational standards of Ahmadis are also much higher: ninety percent of all Ahmadis, and one hundred percent of Ahmadi girls, have at least their matriculation, which is grade ten. The Ahmadis obviously put high stock on education and the acquisition of new knowledge, an impetus which goes back to the founder himself. This is evidenced by the large number of Ahmadis who have, at least amongst the circle that I have met, M. A. degrees. A large number — many of whom have emigrated to Britain and North America — have advanced professional training as doctors, pharmacists, lawyers, engineers and scientists.

We then turned to the discussion of legal matters. He asserted the judgement that the judiciary in Pakistan is corrupt. In the old days this was more commonly found at the lower magistrate's level, but now it is found even at the high court level. The corruption takes the form of intimidation and self-censorship in interpreting the law in any way other than that which is deemed congenial to the regime and, more patently, of taking bribes in rendering decisions on such things as bail.

He recounted an amusing but illuminating case of a maulvi (or mullah, as they are mainly called in the Northwest Frontier) who came to him to take a case which involved the occupation of his land by Bengalis who had entered after the secession of Bangladesh in 1971. The barrister opened and looked at the file which had been brought to him. When the maulvi introduced himself as a prominent member of the intensely anti-Ahmadi Association for the Finality of the Prophet, the barrister closed the file and said: "I think you had better take this to someone else because, as you know, I am an Ahmadi. If I happen to lose the case, you would not feel that I had put out my utmost efforts in your interests. Even if you would think that I had executed your brief to the best of my abilities, I myself would not be certain that I had not been the victim of an underlying reluctance to serve you in the highest possible way. Therefore, I would prefer not to take your case." The maulvi persisted, whereupon the barrister replied that he would take it on the condition that he charge no fee. This the maulvi would not accede to, so that brought the interview to an end. Two months later the maulvi appeared once again and said: "I have been fleeced by various lawyers and still my case seems at the point of losing."

He pleaded that the Ahmadi advocate take it on. He did so and went immediately to the Superintendent and, in presenting the argument, immediately won the case. The maulvi was of course delighted and still comes to visit with some frequency, bringing other clients. What remains to be seen is whether his personal reliance on the competence and honesty of the Ahmadi as a lawyer will translate into a softening of the theological animus against Ahmadis. In this context, we should remember that General Zia ul Haq allegedly used Ahmadi doctors because of their high reputation, even though he was the author of their recent afflictions through his notorious Ordinance XX.

It should be noted that Ahmadi guest houses are the only places in the subcontinent where I have felt free to leave my gear lying around the room while we leave for the day or for several days to visit outlying points. In any other circumstance, including Christian hostels, I would have to take constant, scrupulous care of possessions like money, cameras, pocket-knives, tape recorders, or risk their loss. In these Ahmadi guest houses one has absolutely no fear that one's belongings will be pilfered by the Ahmadi serving staff. Rahmat has left envelopes with large sums of money in his room with complete confidence that all is secure.

5

The Ahmadi Khalifa as Sacred Person

It is common in these days of cross-cultural study of religions to make use of general categories or types in order to classify and make intelligible religious phenomena and activity appearing in different historical traditions.

One such type or interpretive category is that of *sacred man*. Within a large variety of religious communities it is possible to discern the recurring motif of a person or persons with unique status, vocation or responsibility. Thus, throughout the history of religions we may observe religious specialists who function as charismatic prophets who receive authoritative revelations, priests who are custodians of the historic deposit of truth, legal scribes or experts in jurisprudence, experts in ritual practice, and so on.

The general category of sacred person may be exemplified and clarified by observing how the Khalifa functions within the Ahmadi community.

It is difficult for a secularized ethos that predominates in the West to grasp the centrality of the Khalifa in the consciousness of Ahmadis. We can more readily understand the massive impact of rock stars and professional athletes on society than we can that of sacred persons and religious leaders.

In focussing on the Ahmadis it quickly becomes apparent that one cannot understand the community without the Khalifa, nor the Khalifa without his community. They are related as valley and hill; one implies the other.

I first met Hazrat Mirza Tahir Ahmad, grandson of the founder, the Khalifatul Masih IV in our home about fifteen years ago when, though not yet elected to his present office, he was on a tour of Canada. Some of our Ahmadi friends, whose friendship originated in a trek up the Baltoro glacier to K2 in Northern Pakistan in 1975, brought him to our home for a visit.

At the time of our second encounter he had assumed leadership of the Ahmadi Muslims. I was enroute to Pakistan with my friend Rahmat Chawdhry to investigate, in a private research project, the status of Pakistani Ahmadis under the repressive government regime. We stopped in London for a bit less than a week as guests at the headquarters during which time I had two interviews with the Khalifa of about an hour each. I also observed him as he led the prayers in the mosque, and we had a final exchange at the time of our departure.

The impression conveyed by his physical appearance is of a high degree of personal energy and power. He appears of medium height, on the stocky side and powerfully built. The sense of personal vigour is demonstrated by his very swift strides down the length of the mosque, past the assembled participants, as he enters for prayer. At this time, he is accompanied by two bodyguards for fear (the community's, not his) of assassination at the hands of agents of orthodox mullahs. As he leads the prayer or delivers the sermon, he exudes physical strength, moral determination, confidence, authority, and kindliness towards the congregation.

During our interviews (which I taped), he showed himself intelligent and well-read. He was genuinely eager to be informative and utterly candid in response to my questions. I could detect no "impression management" (in the anthropologist Erving Goffman's phrase). This openness and candour had an obvious theological undergirding: so certain are the Ahmadis of divine authority for their understanding of Islam, and so confident of the inevitable triumph of their vision of the truth, that there is no need to dissimulate or placate or manipulate.

Throughout I found him gracious and warm-hearted, and this in spite of my temperamental suspicion of holy men garnered, in part, by my sojourn among gurus and god-men of India. The Khalifa conveyed the authenticity of one who really believes what he says, as it is commonly put. His concern for the well-being of the Ahmadi community was transparent.

During and after my meeting with the Khalifa I have frequently reflected inwardly that if it were one's destiny in life to be part of a religious organization whose authority structure culminates in an individual at its apex, then one could do no better than the Ahmadis. The authority of the institutional office of the Khilafat combines, in my perception, with the authority of a powerful charismatic leader in Mirza Tahir Ahmad. I have pondered how fortunate the Ahmadis are to have this remarkable person as head of their movement, especially at this time of travail but, of course, what I look upon as good fortune, they see as divine providence.

As we were leaving the London headquarters, I asked if I might take a photograph of him. He insisted that a bystander take the shot while he drew me to his side in a gesture at once collegial, paternal and affectionate. Noticing my friend Rahmat standing by and realizing immediately how much it would mean to him, the Khalifa beckoned him to our side for the photograph. He sent for a package to be given to my wife. It contained a gorgeous Pakistani shawl which we prize for itself and for its personal associations.

The tasks of the Khalifatul Masih seem superhuman, in fact, impossible. He is involved in the details of the life of a world-wide community of ten million. He is beseeched to arrange marriages, to counsel on personal crises and needs, to exercise a normative teaching office, and to administer a global missionary and educational organization. A colleague in the School of Architecture at Carleton University recently journeyed to London to present his design for the new Ahmadi mosque in Toronto for the scrutiny of the Khalifa. Many Ahmadis seem weighted with seriousness; he, on the contrary, is joyous and convivial, his enormous responsibilities not-withstanding.

At the Canadian Annual Convention, I observed Hazoor (as he is reverently and affectionately called) as he moved quickly (to say *rushed* might suggest a degree of anxious activity that would belie the poise with which he comports himself) from the car in which we had just been discussing the possibility of CIA infiltration of the Ahmadi movement, to his place in the forefront of the gathered congregation to lead the prayers. Apropos my question: Hazoor does not doubt that CIA infiltration has been attempted, but unsuccessfully. The reason is that the distinctive and cohesive life of the community enables it to identify inauthentic participants.

He appears astonishingly indefatigable; he seems to need no "breathing spaces," no interludes to disengage himself from one strand of discussion in order to insert himself in another discontinuous one.

Not least of the burdens that the Khalifa must bear is the sorrow over the deaths resulting from fidelity to the Ahmadi vision of truth. Since the military regime's promulgation of Ordinance XX in April 1984, the Ahmadis count twenty of their members murdered and at least forty-four since 1974. Coupled with grief over these deaths is the need to exercise a leadership that minimizes threats to the community without compromising obedience to God.

When I remarked upon the intolerable burdens of the Khilafat to Ahmadis, I detected a certain bemused triumph on their faces for what I regard as a humanly impossible task, they perceive as a sign of God's approval of the Ahmadiyya movement. It is, they claim, precisely because the Khalifatul Masih IV is able to fulfil the manifold duties of his office that they remain confident of the divine origin and guidance of their renewal of Islam.

In spite of his staggering workload and the pain of leading a persecuted community, Hazoor retains a gentle but incisive sense of humour. During our dinner table conversation under the great marquee at the Toronto Annual Convention, I remarked on the extraordinary tastiness of our ethnic meal. I lamented that, in spite of our sojourns in the East, my wife had never mastered Pakistani cuisine. He laughed infectiously and then slyly informed me that all the food for the fourteen hundred present had been prepared by a group of men. So much for sexist stereotypes of Muslims! We later visited the garage in which the huge caldrons of tandoori chicken and beef curry and pilau had been cooked on six propane burners — a further testament to the discipline and commitment of the members of the movement.

In summary, we should note that the Khalifa functions as:

(1) Authoritative teacher who clarifies, interprets and applies the revealed message of the Qur'an.

(2) Supreme examplar of the law (*shari'ah*). A *hadith* is seen as applying (with the requisite safeguards) to the Ahmadi Khalifa as well as to Muhammad: God's law forms the individual's character, and the holy individual's personality explains the law.

(3) Object of love and devotion. The response — at once reverential and affectionate — of the community to the person of the Khalifa has to be witnessed to be understood. His sermons are frequently punctuated by cries from the congregation of *Allahu-Akbar* (God is great).

(4) Prayerful interceder. Whether the crisis faced is an impending death, a precarious pregnancy, a retarded child, a dangerous illness, or the need for a marriage partner, the members confidently address their requests for prayer and guidance to the Khalifa.

The love and reverence in which Ahmadis hold their leader is so palpable that I felt a certain embarrassment that I, an outsider, should have had an access to the Khalifa that any one of them would have cherished for a life time and related, until death claimed them, to their grandchildren.

The profound respect with which the Khalifa is regarded devolves even upon immediate family members. My chat in London with the son-in-law of the present Khalifatul Masih IV (and also the son of the third Khalifa) produced an appealing vignette of the domestic life of the Ahmadyya leaders. As a young boy, it had been his practice to wrestle (*kushti*) with his father every morning for exercise. When his father was elected Khalifa, his mother informed the boy that his father was no longer his father and no longer her husband, but Khalifa. As a consequence, the young boy no longer went in the mornings to his father for their accustomed *kushti* sessions. After some time, the father enquired why it was that he no longer visited, whereupon the son replied that it was inappropriate that he wrestle with the Khalifa of the community!

I raised the question how the community's intensity of commitment could be maintained after the passage of a century since the founding of the movement. Extrapolating from my own experience, I detect in the Ahmadis an enthusiasm and tirelessness that is associated with a generation of recent converts. In spite of the tight (ultimately centrally directed) organization of the Ahmadis, the charismatic flush of the movement seems not (in Max Weber's phase) to have suffered *routinization*, that is, a loss of spontaneous excitement in experiencing the truth as part of a unique community serving as the instrument of God's saving purpose in the world.

The answer I am given is that it is the presence of the Khalifa as the concrete personal embodiment of God's authority, guidance and love on earth that maintains the zeal and industriousness of the movement to revitalize and disseminate the true Islam.

6

Conclusion
The Irony of Persecution

A mongst the very few possessions that were left to me by my clergyman father is a medal struck by the then Pope to commemorate the St. Bartholomew Day slaughter of the Hugenots in France, on 24 August 1572. This medal is symbolic of a way of dealing with dissent within the Christian tradition — a way that has tragically marked its past. This is the extirpation of dissident belief by violence and death. Heresy, understood not as out-and-out paganism but as a deviant form of belief within a revealed religious tradition, is regarded as having no rights alongside correct belief. Its elimination is considered to be a holy crusade in the service of God. This type of mentality attains its designation from the events spanning the period from the end of the eleventh to the the end of the thirteenth centuries during which western Christendom sought to regain the holy places from Muslim occupation by launching a church-inspired military campaign, or holy crusade.

What appears to be happening now in Pakistan is the adoption, by a leading and powerful segment of the ulama or Islamic scholars, of a crusading mentality which has generally not been characteristic of the Islamic way of dealing with dissident belief. It is for this reason that I term it metaphorically the "Christianization of Pakistan's Ulama." Let us review the pertinent facts.

The Ahmadis are a group four million strong in Pakistan, and ten million worldwide, who owe their historical origins to the emergence, towards the end of the nineteenth century, of the reformer Mirza Ghulam Ahmad. He claimed to receive revelations from God, including that of his status as the Promised Messiah and the Mahdi which are eschatological figures of divine deliverance within Islam. To these he also added the designation of Prophet although, in his self-undertstanding, the type of prophetic revelation he received was always subordinate to that received by the Prophet Muhammad. Mirza Ghulam Ahmad's prophetic disclosures were mainly in the nature of interpretations of the meaning of the message brought by Muhammad, though they also included predictions about future events. They were not to be viewed as the highest, normative divine revelation, for only Muhammad was the bearer of that.

The founder expressed his understanding of his own subordinate prophetic role in this manner:

> In my view, a person upon whom divine speech, including [knowledge of] the hidden, descends with certainty and in abundance is called a prophet. Therefore Allah called me a prophet, but without a law. The carrier of the law, until the Day of judgement is the Qur'an.

(Cited in Friedmann, p. 134.)

It is of the utmost importance in understanding the Ahmadi conception of prophetic revelation to grasp this claim of Mirza Ghulam Ahmad that he was a prophet without a book and without a law. This, of course, is a crucial distinction since, in Islam, the essence of revelation is scriptural, and the fundamental knowledge which God wishes to disclose to humans is knowledge of his holy will or law for humankind. From the beginning of creation, God has ordained for humans the *shari'ah*— his straight path or holy law — and has purposed to reveal it in a long prophetic succession. What enrages some of Pakistan's ulama is this prophetic claim of Mirza Ghulam Ahmad which they see as a flat contradiction of a cardinal tenet of Islam, namely, the *Khatm-i-Nubuwwat* (finality of the Prophet). Although recognising, in fact, insisting upon, a long historical chain of revelations from God whose essence was always the same, Islam claims that this relevatory process has come to an end in God's disclosures to Muhammad in the seventh century in Arabia. Muhammad is the seal of the prophets in the sense that he confirms the truth of what has gone before; that he corrects misrepresentions and errors that have been allowed to creep into the other revelations, principally those to Christians and Jews; and that he brings to fulfilment preceding prophecies by including knowledge that God did not deem necessary for humankind in a previous age, but which has now become necesssary for their salvation. There are other issues concerning Mirza Ghulam Ahmad's claims for his status as the Promised Messiah that provoke the hostility of the orthodox, but their fundamental objection is to what they perceive to be the Ahmadis' challenge to the finality of prophecy in the person of Muhammad.

The conflict between the Ahmadis and the Sunni ulama may be seen, at one level, as a controversy about the correct interpretation of a conviction that is, in reality, shared by both parties. Both subscribe to the claim that Muhammad is the Seal of the Prophets, that his revelation is the final, authoritative law and book bearing disclosure of what God wants humans to know. The difference is largely a matter of whether God sends authoritative interpreters of that final and normative revelation. If the Promised Messiah had not been instructed by God to use the term *prophet*, perhaps the issue might not have arisen because it is this that is most offensive to doctrinaire Sunni Muslims. In that case, the doctrinal debate might have been more clearly evinced for what I believe it really to be, namely, a difference within the Islamic tradition as to who is the authoritative interpreter of a commonly agreed upon absolute revelation in the Qur'an.

The ulama, it appears, will not allow any deviant interpretations of the Qur'anic disclosure to Muhammad. In this respect, they adopt a position which will surely be confusing to many western observers. A large number of standard western textbooks on Islam will need to be revised if the dogmatic view of the orthodox Pakistani ulama prevails. For in these we find that Islam, contrary to Christianity, stresses *orthopraxy* rather than *orthodoxy*. That is to say, its stress falls not on the adherence with the mind to right ideas or right doctrines about God; rather, the emphasis is on the observance of Islamic life, the practice of certain rituals and moral codes which God has revealed and which are mandatory for human obedience.

This stress on orthopraxy, or right practice, differs from the emphasis in the Christian historical record on orthodoxy, adhering with the mind to right doctrines or beliefs understood to be unreservedly binding upon all members of the church. So fixated have Christians been on right belief or right doctrine that they have been prepared to persecute and annihilate one another for the trespass of believing differently; this we already noted in our reference to the St. Bartholomew Day massacre.

It would seem to an outside observer that the refusal of some of the orthodox ulama to countenance any way of believing differently about the finality of prophetic revelation represents a shift from traditional and norma-tive Islamic perspectives to one that has historically characterized the Christian viewpoint. Far be it for me to intrude upon an internal domestic conflict over the true meaning of Islam. Quite obviously, only Muslims can determine what is true Islam. It does seem, however, that the present policy and practice of the ulama, reinforced by the anti-Ahmadi legislation which strikes the outsider as bizarre, cruel and unjust as he tries to unscramble its meaning and application, violates certain more or less universal perceptions of human dignity and moral obligation.

It is interesting that the Roman Catholic Church, which among Christian bodies persevered for a long time in insisting upon the necessity of adhering to right doctrine, has in more recent years declared the inviolability of conscience and, within certain limits, God's acceptance of those who act in good faith in seeking to obey, love and serve God even though they might be mistaken in certain doctrinal particulars.

There is a peculiar irony in seeking to apply this Islamic norm of orthopraxy, or right conduct, according to God's law to the Ahmadis. In respect of behaviour, the Ahmadis, in my experience, seem to be more observant than the majority of Sunni Muslims. Perhaps in this social factor lies the real source of the orthodox ulama's opposition to the Ahmadis or, if not the source, a strong reinforcement of that hostility.

Almost fifty years ago, Smith had incisively isolated the elements that above all distinguished the Ahmadis from orthodox Muslims. These were to be found not primarily in the field of theology but in sociology. Understanding itself as the new and purified, and hence authentic Islam, the Ahmadis set themselves apart from what they looked upon as degraded and unfaithful Islam. To this they added an internal sense of cohesion, a mutuality of service, and an exhilarating sense of belonging to a divinely empowered missionary fellowship.

Doctrinal differences, of course, there are. In an earlier period these might have centred in Mirza Ghulam Ahmad's claim to embody both the returned Messiah Jesus (strictly speaking: the spiritual and moral qualities possessed by Jesus) and the Mahdi (an eschatological deliverer) — a claim offensive to the orthodox. In contemporary polemics, as we have had frequent occasion to note, the Ahmadis are excoriated by the orthodox mainly for blasphemously denying the finality of Muhammad's prophethood. The Ahmadi insistence on safeguarding the uniqueness and normativeness of Muhammad's status by the qualification that Mirza Ghulam Ahmad was a prophet without a book and without a law, does not seem to soften the orthodox rage against the Ahmadis.

As Smith pointed out the theology of the Ahmadiyya movement is no more heretical than the theology of the respected Agha Khan. It seems reasonable, accordingly, to surmise that the core of the opposition to the Ahmadis lies more in the juxtaposition of two Islamic communities, one led by orthodox mullahs and the other by the Ahmadi Khalifa. The antagonism is no doubt sharpened by the fact that both claim a traditional heritage; the Ahmadis might be perceived as less threatening if they could be dismissed as a modernist reforming group, as they have been misleadingly classified by some observers. Though this designation as modern or liberal might correctly characterize the Lahori off-shoot of the Ahmadyya movement, it does not apply to the main body that has been examined in this study. Smith points out that the basic ethos of the Ahmadiyya movement is traditional. This is certainly confirmed by my encounters with the local jama'ats throughout Pakistan and in Canada.

The Ahmadis disclose a high degree of conservatism in their religious and social practice (ultimately they are the same). They may well be modernists in their opening to modern secular knowledge, in the scientific field especially. They are certainly conservative in their conviction that certain matters of revealed Islamic practice are nonnegotiable and therefore continue to be incumbent upon them. The Ahmadis are strictly observant in prayer. A non-Muslim who spends time amongst them (and wishes to observe their life) must adjust to their religious obligation to pray at the appointed times, the most crippling of which for a non-Muslim is the early rising before one can distinguish clearly the day from the night in order to prepare for the *fajr*, early morning prayer.

The separation of the sexes (*purdah*) is quite strictly practiced; a fact which one might not expect amongst a community that possesses a large number of university graduates, and many trained at the post-graduate level in

CONCLUSION — THE IRONY OF PERSECUTION

western universities. Their view is that the protection and seclusion of women is ordained by God. I never saw a mature female member of the Ahmadi homes in which I stayed in Pakistan. One may visit in their homes for long periods and not be aware of the feminine presence, except for indistinct figures flitting occasionally past doorways, or a knock on a closed door at which time food is to be served by the male host of the household. Though women may be involved in administrative affairs at local jama'at meetings, they are veiled from sight by a curtain and are consulted by questions and answers and comments being addressed to them through the curtain. At some meetings of Canadian Ahmadis, the women, though visibly present, are decorously dressed with long sleeves, and head coverings. In this respect, their practice is probably little different than that prevailing in other mainline Canadian mosques.

At the Canadian Ahmadiyyat Annual Meeting in Toronto during 16-18 June 1989, the sexes were separated for most events. While the Khalifa directly addressed the male audience gathered under an enormous marquee, the women viewed the proceedings on closed circuit television in another tent. During the banquet at the Harbour Castle Westin Hotel, Ahmadi women were seated at the back of the vast dining room during the dinner and separated from the main assembly by a folding partition. Non-Ahmadi women were seated in the conventional western way; my wife, for example, was seated beside me. The partition was removed during the speeches when the hall lights were dimmed and spotlights focussed on the platform holding the head table. The women had requested this arrangement in order to have a session on women's issues with the Khalifa's wife. All this is offered in evidence of the inference that the social life of the Ahmadis is conducted in accordance with traditional views as to what constitutes an Islamic way of life.

If it should turn out that the anti-Ahmadi policy (whether grounded in theology or sociology or both),

105

that manifests itself in discrimination in employment and education, in murders, in judicial penalties of imprisonment and fines for nothing more offensive than declaring oneself to be a Muslim and wearing a kalilmah badge proclaiming the unity of God and the prophethood of Muhammad, is a correct interpretation of Islam, then it will be that many non-Muslims will refuse to entertain the possibility of absolute truth and universal persuasiveness of the Qur'anic revelation. In other words, the anti-Ahmadi ulama, with their present policy, will have been obstacles to respect for Islam and to the propagation of its message. I am strongly persuaded, as an outsider with a long and respectful knowledge of Islam, that the present course of action that has resulted in such hardship for Pakistan Ahmadis represents not an expression of true Islam but an aberration. I had framed the judgement that, occasional *fatawa* or rulings of *kufr* (unbelief) notwithstanding, Islamic society had arrived at a highly pragmatic and humane *modus vivendi* respecting divergent sects, namely, the formula: "He is a Muslim who says he is a Muslim." Though this may be too imprecise to suit some theologians, it did enable the toleration of diversity within the *ummah* (people) of Islam. The present anti-Ahmadi policy in Pakistan is a deviation from that normative consensus. It is helpful to be reminded that if the norms of Islamic identity are to be found pre-eminently in the practice of revealed ritual and revealed rules for moral and social life, then one can scarcely excommunicate the Ahmadis. A hadith (tradition) recording the words of Muhammad brings out the priority of practice over doctrine: "Whoever prays as we pray and turns to our *qiblah* [direction of prayer] and eats what we ritually slaughter is a Muslim." By this behavioural norm, the Ahmadis are solidly Muslim. It is highly likely that the process of secularization of European society with the resulting loss of religious authority, received a powerful impetus from the repugnance generated by the religious persecution and warfare that followed the Protestant reformation of the sixteenth century. Similarily, the orthodox ulama's reaction against the peaceful Ahmadis can only serve to harden and justify a western bias against Islam and stiffen the resolve of those anti-Islamic forces within the Islamic world itself.

For those who are Muslims, this little book is an invitation to cleanse Islam of the blight that is represented by the persecution of the Ahmadis that I have sketched in these pages. How can this harsh and deadly assault on the Ahmadis be compatible with the vision of an Islamic society? Let the opposition to Ahmadyyat be transferred from the field of violence and imprisonment to that of theological disputation and competition in communal holiness in obedience to God's revealed law.

For non-Muslims, whose concerns are not Islamic authenticity but elementary human justice, this study is an appeal to exert their influence on the government of Pakistan to reject co-option by the fanatical mentality exhibited by certain conservative and fundamentalist theologians and jurists within Islam. The use of the punitive apparatus of a modern state to deny a peaceful group its right of self-definition violates the convictions concerning a natural order of rights and freedoms that, even if sometimes transgressed in practice, have become enshrined in the social philosophy of all the nations of the world which have endorsed the United Nations Universal Declaration of Human Rights.

Appendix I

Interview with the Author

The following is a transcription of an interview with Dr. Antonio R. Gualtieri conducted by Peter Meggs, host of the radio program Open House, *and aired over the Canadian Broadcasting Corporation network on 20 March 1988. It covers much of the same ground as the preceding text, but in a condensed and more colloquial style, and for that very reason may serve as a handy introduction to or resumé of the book.*

Peter Meggs: Dr. Gualtieri, the Ahmadis consider themselves Muslim. Why does Islam condemn them as heretics?

Antonio R. Gualtieri: I think this is the problem between self-definition and definition from outside. The Ahmadis themselves, as you said, do regard themselves as Muslims. More than that, they regard themselves as true Muslims. They feel that the reformist renewal movement that started towards the end of the nineteenth century was the rebirth of true Islam.

PM: Tell me something about that movement that got them going.

ARG: Well, it centres on a particular charismatic figure. His name is Mirza Ghulam Ahmad who was from a prominent family in Qadian. This is in the Punjab, now a part of India. He had spiritual experiences. He was a scholarly sort — he read the Qur'an and other religious texts diligently. His interpretation was that God spoke to him and let him know that he was the Promised Messiah and Mahdi, a figure in Islamic thought about the last days. He is the "rightly guided one" who will come at the end of the age to restore the religion of Islam and justice.

The Messiah — which might strike Christians as odd— is also a Muslim figure. Orthodox Islam has also assimilated the notion that (according to some of the mythology or stories) at some point in God's future, toward the end of time, the Messiah will come again to do God's work — to destroy unbelieving Christians and, basically, to renew Islam before the final judgement. Mirza Ghulam Ahmad thought that he was the fulfilment of those Islamic prophecies, that he was in his own person both Mahdi, the "rightly guided one," and the Promised Messiah.*

PM: Traditional Islam did not go along with that?

ARG: No, it did not. They might not have had so much trouble with that, for there has been a great deal of dissent within Islam — contrary to some of our notions of its monolithic quality. What I think really tipped the balance against Ghulam Ahmad was his self-designation as a prophet. That ran in the face of Islamic orthodoxy that asserts that prophetic revelation ceased with the advent of Muhammad. There was a long succession of prophets, such as Jesus and Abraham, through whom God spoke to the world in the past. In the last days, that is, in the seventh century of the Christian era, God sent His final prophet and that was Muhammad. By calling himself a prophet, Ghulam Ahmad ran the risk of a serious misunderstanding.

PM: Isn't there a similar problem between Islam and the Baha'i on that kind of issue?

---

* Hindsight allows me to obviate a possible error. Ahmad himself preached a non-violent struggle or jihad in the promulgation of Islam. Whereas he relied on preaching and persuasion to advance Islam in the face of its opponents, some of Ahmad's orthodox critics insisted that jihad in the cause of Islam entailed force and bloodshed. This is one of the issues that divided Ahmadis from Sunni theologians.

ARG: That is right. There are latter-day charismatic spiritual leaders who emerge who usually view themselves as renewing Islam, and who make claims for the authority of their message. This suggests that they are denying or violating that fundamental Muslim tenet of the finality of prophecy in Muhammad. I should quickly break in here to say that this is the way orthodox Muslims see this movement. They see it as a movement that originates in a prophetic claim that is heretical. The Ahmadis themselves are more subtle about their understanding of what occurred in the prophecies or revelations given to their founder.

Ahmad himself claimed that he was a prophet without a book and without a law. If one understands Islam, one understands that revelation in Islam is quintessentially scriptural. It is in a book. You have the Evangel of Jesus or the Torah of Moses. The essence of that scripture revelation is law. God is not interested in giving a lot of information about His metaphysical nature; He is interested in conveying a law which informs people how to live their lives compatible with the divine will. So when Ghulam Ahmad says: "I am a prophet without a law and without a book"— he is definitely subordinating himself to the definitive divine authority of Muhammad. But the orthodox did not see it that way.

PM: We are talking about the nineteenth century, aren't we?

ARG: The date they use for the emergence of the movement as a community is 1889.

PM: Although there are ten million Ahmadis worldwide, in Pakistan they are outlawed, are they not?

ARG: What has happened in Pakistan is very interesting and it is that which drove me to Pakistan to do this research. I am interested in the problem of self-definition; that is, how people regard themselves and how others look upon them.

In 1974, when Zulfiqar Bhutto was still in power, the National Assembly of Pakistan made an amendment to the constitution that defined the Ahmadis as non-Muslims. It is very peculiar that outsiders were not content, simply to say: "You are not a good or true Muslim." Muslims, after all, have been saying that to one another for a long time, just as Christians have. They now said: "You are not allowed to understand yourself as a Muslim."

Of course, Ahmadis do, in the depths of their souls with a fervour that I have scarcely seen repeated elsewhere, understand themselves as Muslims.

PM: What does that mean to the Ahmadis when that was said by Bhutto back in 1974? Does that bring persecution to them?

ARG: It certainly did.

PM: What kind of persecution?

ARG: There have been popular disturbances throughout the last century. There was a disturbance with intensity in 1953 that generated the well-known Munir report on the subject, and then further disturbances in the 1970s that moved the National Assembly to decree the Ahmadis "non-Muslims." That process of marginalization, harassment and persecution, I think, culminates with the military ordinances of General Zia ul Haq.

PM: The president now.

ARG: Yes, although there has been the rescinding of martial law, at least in theory. Under General Zia, the anti-Ahmadi legislation has intensified so that if an Ahmadi calls himself or herself a Muslim or calls his or her place of worship a mosque or gives the *azan*, the call to prayer which is standard for Muslim ritual worship, and in any other way outrages the feelings of Muslims, that person is liable to three years in prison and a fine. I visited a prison in Baluchistan and talked to four Ahmadis who were in prison for a year for the offence of wearing the kalimah badge. *Kalimah tayyabah* is a formula that states the standard Muslim profession of faith: "There is no God but God and Muhammad is His prophet." If an Ahmadi wears that, he or she is accused under Statute 298(c) of the Pakistan penal code of posing as a Muslim. It is as if, for example, you made certain Christian affirmations and, on the basis of my prejudgements, I said that you cannot

112

really be a Christian but are simply pretending to be one. When Ahmadis do what any devout Muslim would want to do, namely, pray, to profess the unity of God and the prophethood of Muhammad, to go on a pilgrimage, they are accused of pretending to be Muslims — a crime which is covered in the penal code.

PM: Does that apply to all the five pillars of Islam? If they practise any of them, are they accused of heresy?

ARG: They are not only accused of heresy. That is all right — religious people are accustomed to calling one another heretics. They are also accused of being criminals, of violating the law of the land. For instance, in one case, a person had a charge brought against him by some mullah (an orthodox religious leader) because he had said the *Durood-Ibrahim* (a kind of prayer that prays that God's blessings that were given to Abraham, Isaac and Jacob will also be given to the prophet). This person was accused of pretending to be a Muslim and was charged. The people who heard this prayer were also charged with posing to be Muslims. Some of them are out on bail; some, as I have already pointed out, are in prison.

PM: What form does this persecution take in Pakistan?

ARG: Besides imprisonment of people, discrimination in jobs (they are not promoted), their children cannot get into university, even kindergarten. In addition to the assassinations which, as I said, were inspired by certain fundamentalist pirs and mullahs, you also see their sacred buildings defaced or, in some cases, destroyed. In Mardan the mosque was utterly destroyed. In other towns — in Quetta, in Hyderabad, in Gujranwala — the mosques have been sealed by the authorities. In order to maintain law and order — to prevent a mass uprising so the argument runs — they simply put padlocks on some of these Ahmadi mosques and post soldiers there so that the Ahmadis are obliged to worship in homes. The sealing of the mosques does not seem to impede their worship. They simply move off to homes. Sometimes they are harassed there, being told that they are transforming homes into public places of worship, so they will move to other homes. Their cemeteries have had tombstones altered by the Ahmadis themselves in conformity to the law. They are told they are not allowed to put certain Muslim inscriptions on their tombstones. If you visit the cemeteries, you will see where these have all had to be removed. They have had to remove the word *masjid* (mosque) from their places of worship because, according to the law, their Ahmadi places of worship cannot be mosques. If they insist on using that term, they are accused of pretending to be that which they are not — Muslims. You can see it in the restrictions on their places of worship, as well as on their persons.

PM: What kind of threat does this coercion pose to traditional Islam?

ARG: That is where we are in the world today. For the people of fundamentalist persuasion, it is not a threat to Islam. It is the way of securing and protecting the purity of Islam. From a different perspective (which would be my own), I think it is a blight on Islam. My understanding of Islam is that, although no religion is perfect in this respect, it has a better record than Christians or Jews on the question of toleration of other faiths. I think what is happening in Pakistan is at best an embarrassment to good Pakistani Muslims of sound sense with an understanding of their tradition and, at worst, it is kind of a demonic, inhuman attack on a community. I mentioned imprisonment. That is the least severe of the punishments. There have been murders in shops. A prominent opthamologist was killed in Hyderabad. I would say that in Sind alone probably twenty people have been killed, and in Pakistan maybe thirty or forty. Assassinations such as these are inspired by super-orthodox fundamentalist mullahs, or religious leaders, who think they are protecting Islam against these heretical pollutions. The police, to the best of my knowledge, do nothing about bringing assassins to court. The cases are not prosecuted.

PM: You mentioned Christianity a moment ago. I think I read somewhere that the Ahmadis have beliefs that are related to Christianity and Hinduism.

114

ARG: Very interesting. Since we are close to Good Friday, it is germane to say that they have this intriguing doctrine of Christ's death. Christians, of course, affirm that Jesus died on the cross. It is absolutely essential for Christians to affirm that this is the way God redeems humankind. As you know, Jesus is in the Qur'an, the holy book of Islam. Jesus, according to orthodox Islam, did not die on the cross, but either a double or someone else died in His stead. Jesus was supernaturally raised up to God, like the Christian doctrine of the ascension.

PM: Is that because they could not believe that God Himself would die in that fashion?

ARG: Well, not quite that because for Muslims, of course, Jesus would never be God. Perhaps the largest and most critical objection Muslims have to Christians is that they have taken a human person and ascribed to this person divine qualities. For Muslims that is the most heinous sin against God. Rather, they feel that God would not abandon the prophet. It would be counter to God's protection of His holy prophets to allow Jesus, the prophet, to die on the cross. God triumphs — He raises Jesus up to heaven and those who are faithful to Him are ultimately vindicated.

PM: You were going to tell me about the Ahmadis' belief in the crucifixion.

ARG: Yes. The Ahmadis hold, like orthodox Muslims, that Jesus did not die on the cross but, unlike the orthodox Muslims, they deny His supernatural ascension to heaven from which He will return as Messiah at the end of the age. The Ahmadis say that Jesus retired eastward to seek out and preach to the lost tribes of Israel, and died in Kashmir. They have His tomb in Kashmir. At that point, they are denying Christian claims that He died on the cross and are denying orthodox Muslim claims that He was supernaturally raised up to God. That is another point of dissension. I mentioned the most important point — the finality of prophethood in Muhammad— Muhammad being the seal or last of the prophets.

PM: How are they related to Hinduism?

ARG: Negatively and positively. One of the reasons that I think explains the emergence of Ghulam Ahmad in the late nineteenth century was a reaction to Christian missionaries and also to a renascent Hinduism. Ghulam Ahmad was trying to reassert what he thought were superior claims of Islam against Hindu preaching. They are also related in a positive way in that Ghulam Ahmad claimed not only to be the Ahmadi, the "rightly guided one" that was expected to restore religion and justice at the end of time, and not only the Promised Messiah that Christians, Jews and orthodox Muslims anticipate, but claimed also to be an *avatar*, an incarnation of Lord Vishnu, one of the prominent Hindu dieties.

PM: He made very wide claims then.

ARG: Yes, he did. There is no doubt that, in trying to understand the Ahmadis, one cannot mask the centrality of the charasmatic leader — not only the founder but even today. In London, England I visited the Khalifa, the spiritual leader of the community who is now in exile in London because his life would be in peril in Pakistan. I was moved and astonished to see the devotion that the devotees gave to the Khalifa. It is a community which is vibrant, highly trained (it has a hundred percent literacy rate), and has a very active missionary outreach in West Africa, Indonesia, and all over the world.

PM: I do not think of Muslims as being people who go out to convert others, but the Ahmadis do.

ARG: Yes. I think Islam itself, of whatever persuasion, is a missionary movement.

PM: The Ahmadis, having ten million around the world, seem to be very, very successful as missionaries.

ARG: You are absolutely right. They are missionary minded, even beyond the expansion of ordinary Sunni, or orthodox Islam. All Muslims want to propogate what they consider to be the true and final revelation of God. But the Ahmadis do so with a particular intensity. In Rabwah, Pakistan, I visited their missionary college where even in these times when it is difficult for foreign Ahmadis to get visas into Pakistan, there are still students

116

from Nigeria, Uganda, Ghana, Indonesia, United States, and Britain who train to be missionaries and who make this a lifetime vocation. Outside London they have an enormous missionary printing enterprise where they translate the Qur'an and writings of the founder and other theological works of the movement into myriad languages. It is a translation work which reminds me of Christian translation work, such as is done particularly by the conservative Christian groups. They are highly organized and highly disciplined. They are very generous in the giving of their money to the movement. It is a movement which seems not to have lost that first flush of enthusiasm that revitalization movements in religion usually have.

PM: Has it not been almost a century since they started?

ARG: Right. When I ask them the reason for their enthusiasm, they say it is because they have the living presence of the Khalifa. They feel that this enthusiasm, this level of dedication, would not persist were it not that they have a divinely guided leader who handles almost all the ongoing affairs of the community. One of our architects at Carleton University is designing a new Ahmadi mosque in Toronto. He flew over to London to lay the plans before the Khalifa. I simply do not know how a simple human being has those resources of energy to attend to all the miniscule details of a worldwide community but so it is.

PM: What is happening to that worldwide community? Are other Muslim countries condemning the Ahmadis as heretics as well?

ARG: I think the condemnation is pretty well worldwide in my experience.

PM: Persecution too?

ARG: No. I am not acquainted with all of the facts. It would be necessary there to make a sound statement. My impression so far is that harassment which then becomes persecution is expanding around the world because fundamentalism is in, whether it be Christian, Judaic or Islamic fundamentalism. In Pakistan I think the government has made political mileage by aligning itself with the desires and designs of the fundamentalist mullahs. The easy way to appear to be super-Islamic —that is, as I say, politically advantageous today— is to pick on the Ahmadis. I think that maltreatment of Ahmadis exists in other countries as well, although it seems to exist with particular virulence in present-day Pakistan.

PM: What do the fundamentalist mullahs in Iran think of the Ahmadis?

ARG: The Shi'ites themselves are already accustomed to being somewhat on the outside with respect to Sunni Islam. I would expect that the relationships are not so acrimonious as they are with Sunni countries. In the case of Saudi Arabia, some have speculated that the intensity of Pakistan's governmental opposition to the Ahmadis is generated not only by a collusion with the fundamentalist mullahs in order to allow the government to appear dedicatedly Islamic and therefore attractive to the religious masses, but is also motivated by a desire to acquiesce in Saudi Arabia's designs to be the orthodox spokesman or custodian of Islamic purity. Islam in Pakistan receives funding from Saudi Arabia. The gigantic new Shah Faisal mosque located in Islamabad has been built largely with Saudi money.

PM: What will happen in the future? They seem to be growing faster than Islam itself?

ARG: I am not sure what the future holds. From the point of view of the Ahmadis themselves, they are very optimistic. They feel they are in true line of fidelity to the Qur'an, to Muhammad, with the additional inspiration of their founder and the present-day Khalifa. They are supremely confident that the future belongs to them and their version of Islam.

PM: Is it that kind of confidence that makes them so attractive?

ARG: I asked this question persistently. I travelled all over Pakistan. I have never travelled so much as on this last trip to Pakistan. I would ask: "How are you viewed by your neighbours? How do the people you work with, or have to do business with, regard you? Are they distancing themselves from you lest they be contaminated by charges of associating with criminal and heretical Ahmadis?"

The answer was: "No, the relationships with immediate neighbours are very good. The neighbours come to Ahmadi weddings. The opposition is mainly official and stirred up by particular pirs, holy men or mullahs, who incite mobs usually belonging to super-fundamentalist youth organizations or an association for the protection of the finality of the prophet. The relations with immediate neighbours are convivial; they are respected. It is said that General Zia uses Ahmadi doctors because they are well trained and regarded as incorruptible. Because Ahmadi lawyers have a reputation for giving the best possible service, they have as their clients fundamentalist leaders. They are well regarded by the ordinary people in Pakistan.

PM: Very, very interesting. I am very grateful to you for coming in and telling us about the Ahmadis. I have been speaking with Dr. Antonio Gualtieri, Professor of Religion at Carleton University, Ottawa. Thank you again.

Appendix II

Passport Declaration
in Case of Muslims

I, _____ S/o_____ aged____years, adult Muslim, resident of......... hereby solemnly declare that:

(i) I am a Muslim and believe in the absolute and un-qualified finality of the prophethood of Muhammad (peace be upon him) the last of the prophets.

(ii) I do not recognize any person who claims to be a prophet in any sense of the word or of any description whatsoever after Muhammad (peace be upon him) or recognize such a claimant as a prophet or a religious reformer as a Muslim.

(iii) I consider Mirza Ghulam Ahmad Qadiani to be an imposter nabi and also consider his followers whether belonging to the Lahori or Qadiani group, to be non-Muslim.

Date_____   Signature or
                               thumb impression.

Appendix III

Conditions of Bai'at (Initiation) in Ahmadiyya Movement in Islam
By
Hazrat Mirza Ghulam Ahmad of Qadian
The Promised Messiah and Mahdi
(Peace be upon him)

I. The initiate shall solemnly promise that he shall abstain from Shirk (association of any partner with God) right upto the day of his death.

II. That he shall keep away from falsehood, fornication, adultery, tresspasses of the eye, debauchery, dissipation, cruelty, dishonesty, mischief and rebellion; and will not permit himself to be carried away by passions, however strong they may be.

III. That he shall regularly offer the five daily prayers in accordance with the commandments of God and the Holy Prophet; and shall try his best to be regular in offering the Tahajjud (pre-dawn supererogatory prayers) and invoking Darood (blessings) on the Holy Prophet; that he shall make it his daily routine to ask forgiveness for his sins, to remember the bounties of God and to praise and glorify Him.

IV. That under the impulse of any passions, he shall cause no harm whatsoever to the creatures of Allah, in general, and Muslims, in particular, neither by his tongue nor by his hands nor by any other means.

V. That he shall remain faithful to God in all circumstances of life, in sorrow and happiness, adversity and prosperity, in felicity and trials; and shall in all conditions remain resigned to the decree of Allah and keep himself ready to face all kinds of indignities and sufferings in His way and shall never turn away from it at the onslaught of any misfortune; on the contrary, he shall march forward.

VI. That he shall refrain from following un-Islamic customs and lustful inclinations, and shall completely submit himself to the authority of the Holy Qur'an; and shall make the word of God and the sayings of the Holy Prophet the guiding principles in every walk of his life.

VII. That he shall entirely give up pride and vanity and shall pass all his life in lowliness, humbleness, cheerfulness, forbearance and meekness.

VIII. That he shall hold faith, the honour of faith, and the cause of Islam dearer to him than his life, wealth, honour, children and all other dear ones.

IX. That he shall keep himself occupied in the service of God's creatures, for His sake only; and shall endeavour to benefit mankind to the best of his God-given abilities and powers.

X. That he shall enter into a bond of brotherhood with this humble servant of God, pledging obedience to me in everything good, for the sake of Allah, and remain faithful to it till the day of his death; that he shall exert such a high devotion in the observance to this bond as is not to be found in any other worldly relationship and connections demanding devoted dutifulness.

Ishtehar Takmeel-e-Tabligh,
12 January 1889.

Bibliography

Abbott, Freeland (1968) *Islam and Pakistan*. Ithaca: Cornell University Press.

Adams, Charles (1987) "Article Jama'at-i-Islami," in *The Enclycopedia of Religion*. Ed. Mircea Eliade. New York: MacMillan Publishing Company.

Ahmad, Mirza Bashir-ud-din Mahmud (1980) *Invitation to Ahmadiyyat*. London: Routledge & Kegan Paul.

Ahmad, Mirza Ghulam (1898) *Kashf-ul-Ghita*. Lahore: Victoria Press.

Ahmad, Mirza Tahir (1989) *Murder in the Name of Allah*. Cambridge: Lutterworth Press.

Binder, Leonard (1963) *Religion and Politics in Pakistan*. Berkley and Los Angeles: University of California Press.

Brush, Stanley E. (1987) Article "Ahmadiyah" in *The Encyclopedia of Religion*. Ed.Mircea Eliade. New York:Macmillan Publishing Company.

Friedmann, Yohannan (1989) *Prophecy Continuous: Aspects of Ahmadi Religious Thought and its Medieval Background*. Berkeley: University of California Press.

Houtsma, M.T. (1953) Article "Ahmadiya" in *Shorter Encyclopaedia of Islam*. Eds., H.A.R. Gibb and J.H. Kramers. Leiden: E.J. Brill.

Khan, Muhammad Zafrulla (1978) *Ahmadiyyat: The Renaissance of Islam*. London: Tabshir Publications.

_____(1983) *Servant of God: A Personal Narrative*. Old Woking, Surrey: Unwin Bros.

Lavan, Spencer (1974) *The Ahmadiyah Movement: A History and Perspective*. New Delhi: Manohar Book Service.

Mann, W.E. (1955) *Sect, Cult and Church in Alberta*. Toronto: University of Toronto Press.

Munir, Muhammad (1954) *Report of the Court of Inquiry constituted under Punjab Act II of 1954 to enquire into the*

Punjab Disturbances of 1953. Lahore: Superintendent, Government Printing, Punjab.

_____ (1980) *From Jinnah to Zia.* Lahore: Vanguard Books Ltd.

Parker, Karen (1987) *Human Rights in Pakistan.* San Francisco: Human Rights Advocates, Inc.

Parvez, Ghulam Ahmad (1969) "Fatwas of Kufr," *Tulu-i-Islam* (August). Lahore.

Petren, Gustaf, et.al.(1987) *Pakistan: Human Rights After Martial Law.* Geneva:International Commission of Jurists.

Smith, Wilfred Cantwell (1946) *Modern Islam in India: A Social Analysis.* Lahore: Sh. Muhammad Ashraf.

_____ (1960) Article "Ahmadiyya" in *The Encylopaedia of Islam* (New Edition). Leiden: E.J. Brill.

_____ (1963) *The Meaning and End of Religion: A New Approach to the Religious Traditions of Mankind.* New York: Macmillan Publishing Co.

Troeltsch, Ernst (1960) *The Social Teaching of the Christian Church.* Trans. Olive Wyon. New York: Harper.

Antonio R. Gualtieri is Professor of Religion, Carleton University in Ottawa, Canada. Besides graduate degrees in Theology he holds a Ph.D. in History of Religions from McGill University. His interests lie in problems of religious diversity, comparative religious ethics, and method and theory in the study of religion. Previously he served as a minister of The United Church of Canada and taught in the Religion Department at Vassar College. Among the journals in which his articles have appeared are : *SR Studies, Studies in Religion/Sciences Religieuses, Scottish Journal of Theology, Religious Theological Studies, Encounter, Religion and Society, Journal of Dharma, Journal of Ecumenical Studies, Canadian Ethnic Studies, Dalhousie Review, and the Journal of the American Academy of Religion.* He is also the author of : *Christianity and Native Traditions : Indigenization and Syncretism Among the Inuit and Dene of the Western Arctic* and *The Vulture and the Bull : Religious Responses to Death.* He has been married to Peggy Nixon for thirty-four years and they are the parents of three daughters and a son.